THE MODERN TEMPER

Joseph Wood Krutch was born in Knoxville, Tennessee, in 1893. He was graduated from the University of Tennessee and received his Ph.D. from Columbia University in 1923. He became the drama critic of the *Nation* in 1925, and in 1937 was appointed Professor of English (later Brander Matthews Professor of Dramatic Literature) at Columbia. In the early 'fifties he resigned both posts and moved to Arizona where he now lives. He is the author of many books, among them: Our Changing Morals (1925); Five Masters (1930); The American Drama Since 1918 (1939); Samuel Johnson (1944); Henry David Thoreau (1948); The Twelve Seasons (1949); The Desert Year (1952); and The Measure of Man (1954). His most recent volume is The Voice of the Desert (1955).

The
Modern
Temper

A STUDY AND A CONFESSION

BY JOSEPH WOOD KRUTCH

*

A HARVEST BOOK
Harcourt, Brace & World, Inc.
New York

To my Brother
Charles E. Krutch

There is a game for players still to play,
Pretending that the board was never lost,
But still the painted counters will decay
And knowledge sit alone to count the cost.

MARK VAN DOREN

CONTENTS

This book was first published early in 1929. Its thesis would no doubt have been described as Existentialist, if the word had then been in popular use, and the thesis was this:

The universe revealed by science, especially the sciences of biology and psychology, is one in which the human spirit cannot find a comfortable home. That spirit breathes freely only in a universe where what philosophers call Value Judgments are of supreme importance. It needs to believe, for instance, that right and wrong are real, that Love is more than a biological function, that the human mind is capable of reason rather than merely of rationalization, and that it has the power to will and to choose instead of being compelled merely to react in the fashion predetermined by its conditioning. Since science has proved that none of these beliefs is more than a delusion, mankind will be compelled either to surrender what we call its humanity by adjusting to the real world or to live some kind of tragic existence in a universe alien to the deepest needs of its nature.

Most of the political and military events which have shaken our world took place after 1929. I cannot claim to have prophesied them in detail, and what many believe to be the downfall of our civilization sometimes seems to be approaching faster than I thought it would —though I did suggest, even in 1929, that some barbarians would probably invade a civilization which lost the faith by which it had lived and that Russia seemed the most likely place from which such barbarians would come.

More than a quarter of a century later I find myself asking three questions: (1) Do educated people continue to believe that science has exposed as delusions those convictions and standards upon which Western civilization was founded? (2) Is the ultimate cause of the catastrophe with which that civilization is threatened this loss of faith in humanity itself? (3) Is it really true, as I once believed, that there is no escaping the scientific demonstration that religion, morality, and the human being's power to make free choices are all merely figments of the imagination?

To the first two of these questions the answer still seems to me to be "Yes." Despite the so-called revival of popular religion which amounts to little more than the acceptance of the church as a social institution and despite a perhaps increasingly strong undercurrent of psychological and sociological protest against determinism and relativism, the most prevalent educated opinion is still that men are animals and that animals are machines. One kind of intellectual may respond to this conviction by embracing the creed of atheistical Existentialism which is the tragic solution proposed in *The Modern Temper*. A larger group turns optimistically toward experimental psychology, the techniques for sociological conditioning, and the methods of indoctrination developed by the manipulators of the media of mass communication and hopes from them for the creation of a Robot Utopia whose well-adjusted citizens will have comfortably forgotten that their forefathers believed themselves to be Men.

But neither the one group nor the other rejects the assumption that Western men, traditionally endowed with reason, will, and a valid sense of value, is an exploded myth. And because this conviction still prevails among educated men I still believe it true that it poses the most serious of all threats to our civilization and is, indeed, the ultimate source of most of our specific dilemmas—as it is, for instance of our dilemma in the face of communism which embodies the really logical conclusion to be drawn from the premises which so many nominally anticommunists share with their formal opponents.

Exactly twenty-five years after *The Modern Temper* appeared I returned to the general subject in a book called *The Measure of Man*. In it I attempted to set forth my reasons for no longer believing that the mechanistic, materialistic, and deterministic conclusions of science do have to be accepted as fact and hence as the premises upon which any philosophy of life or any estimate of man and his future must be based. This book has been called a "reply" to *The Modern Temper* but it is that only in a limited sense. The latter had been subtitled "A Study and a Confession"; its successor might well have been described as "A Study and a Refutation." The modern temper itself has developed somewhat, especially in the direction of that attempted "adjustment" to dismal assumptions which makes Social Engineering rather than Existentialist resignation the dominant religion of today. But the description which I gave of its origins and the consequences likely to follow from it seem to me as valid as they ever were. It is only my own attitude toward it which is different. What I described and shared in I still describe but no longer accept. Hence the situation which *The Modern Temper* presents as hopeless does not now seem to me entirely so. But by the diagnosis I will still stand.

1956 JOSEPH WOOD KRUTCH

The chapters into which the book is divided are in reality sections of a single long essay which was written largely for my own satisfaction and which grew out of an effort to understand myself. I hoped to reduce to definite form those floating convictions, tendencies, and moods which, taken together, constitute a temperament, and, since the intellectual atmosphere in which that temperament was formed seems to me the one most characteristic of our time, I ventured to assume that there is something characteristic about my reactions to it. I know that I have learned the same things and thought about the same problems as most of my contemporaries. I know further, both from the books which they have written and from the words which some few of them have spoken to me, that I have felt myself carried in a general direction which kept me side by side with many of them, and because of this fact I have ventured to give the essay the title which it bears.

The book is at once a study and a confession—a study of the various tendencies in contemporary thought and a confession of the mood which submission to these tendencies has engendered. In so far as it states what these tendencies are, it is, I believe, objective; in so far as it treats of the emotional states which these tendencies produced, it is, of necessity, colored by an individual personality, and yet the effort has been, even where these are concerned, to deal only with those emotional attitudes which bear a strong family resemblance to those which are common to many. Here are, at least, no private adventures, no purely individual experiences, but only the thoughts engendered by the contemplation of the facts and theories familiar to every reading person and stated in a form as detached as I was capable of achieving. If the essay cannot escape being personal, it is at least as little so as I have been able to make it, and whatever value it may have comes from the fact that, though doubtless few people will accept all its conclusions or sign all the articles of its confession of faith, yet many, I believe, will recognize its problems as their own and its mood as one which at moments, at least, they have shared.

In the effort to describe and account for this mood which I recognized in myself and of which some aspect or other seemed to me to be reflected in innumerable books of various sorts, I have been compelled to make reference to many facts or supposed facts in biology, psychology, and anthropology. Obviously no person is qualified to assert them all with authority and obviously I am much less qualified than many others, but when I state them I do so not as facts but simply as commonplaces which we have been taught to believe. My subject is not any series of objective fact, but a state of mind, and in the effort to describe and account for it I am responsible not for Truth but for the convictions, scientific or otherwise, which I and my contemporaries have been led to hold. If God never existed it is nevertheless certain that a belief that he did had an effect upon the mood of the Middle Ages hardly less great than any really existing God could have had, and if the tenets of Freudianism or the hypotheses of the Darwinian theory are false, they have at least been so accepted as to influence the modern temper quite as unmistakably as if they were true. I do not, for instance, know that the sexuality of savages is far less tyrannical than that of civilized people; neither, for that matter, do I actually know that the earth goes around the sun. But I do know that both these things have been asserted by learned and intelligent people to whom I and my fellows have listened, and I do know further that both these supposed facts have an emotional significance. That is as far as it is necessary to go if they are to be used as I use them, only in the effort to account for a mood.

Beyond this I can say only that in the ensuing pages I have tried to be as candid as possible, to follow out every thought as far as I could without caring where it would lead and without tempering any conclusions out of consideration to either my own sensibilities or those of anyone else. I have neither celebrated the good old days nor attempted to prove that mankind is about to enter upon its golden age. I am sure that those who hold conventional religious opinions will find my book in many ways offensive and I fancy that many who are militantly rationalistic will be disgusted by my failure to share their optimism concerning the future of a rationalistic humanity. But though I am sensible of the fact that it would be ironical indeed if, by displeasing both these groups, a book which purported to describe the modern temper should find no one willing to acknowledge the attitude which it holds to be typical, that must be as it will. Certainly if any modern temper like that herein described does actually exist it is very different from that scientific optimism which, though it is being widely popularized at the present moment, really belongs to nineteenth-century thought, and certainly one of its most distinguishing features is just its inability to achieve either religious belief on the one hand or exultant atheism on the other. Unlike their grandfathers, those who are its victims do not and never expect to believe in God; but unlike their spiritual fathers, the philosophers and scientists of the nineteenth century, they have begun to doubt that rationality and knowledge have any promised land into which they may be led. That is, perhaps, the most general form in which their dilemma may be stated.

Several sections of the essay appeared in the *Atlantic Monthly*. I wish to give my thanks to the editor of that magazine for permission to reprint them here in their proper place.

JOSEPH WOOD KRUTCH

THE MODERN TEMPER

in protest to cause the entire world in so far as he knows it—his nurse or his parents—to rush to his aid. The whole of his physical universe is obedient to his will and he is justified by his experience in believing that his mere volition controls his destiny. Only as he grows older does he become aware that there are wills other than his own or that there are physical circumstances rebellious to any human will. And only after the passage of many years does he become aware of the full extent of his predicament in the midst of a world which is in very few respects what he would wish it to be.

As a child he is treated as a child, and such treatment implies much more than the physical coddling of which Freud speaks. Not only do those who surround him co-operate more completely than they ever will again to satisfy his wishes in material things, but they encourage him to live in a spiritual world far more satisfactory than their own. He is carefully protected from any knowledge of the cruelties and complexities of life; he is led to suppose that the moral order is simple and clear, that virtue triumphs, and that the world is, as the desires of whole generations of mankind have led them to try to pretend that it is, arranged according to a pattern which would seem reasonable and satisfactory to human sensibilities. He is prevented from realizing how inextricably what men call good and evil are intertwined, how careless is Nature of those values called mercy and justice and righteousness which men have come, in her despite, to value; and he is, besides, encouraged to believe in a vast mythology peopled with figments which range all the way from the Saints to Santa Claus and which represent projections of human wishes which the adult has come to recognize as no more than projections but which he is willing that the child, for the sake of his own happiness, should believe real. Aware how different is the world which experience reveals from the world which the spirit desires, the mature, as though afraid that reality could not be endured unless the mind had been gradually inured to it, allow the child to become aware of it only by slow stages, and little by little he learns, not only the limitations of his will, but the moral discord of the world. Thus it is, in a very important sense, true that the infant does come trailing clouds of glory from that heaven which his imagination creates, and that as his experience accumulates he sees it fade away into the light of common day.

Now races as well as individuals have their infancy, their adolescence, and their maturity. Experience accumulates not only from year to year but from generation to generation, and in the life of each person it plays a little larger part than it did in the life of his father. As civilization grows older it too has more and more facts thrust upon its consciousness and is compelled to abandon one after another, quite as the child does, certain illusions which have been dear to it. Like the child, it has instinctively assumed that what it would like to be true is true, and it never gives up any such belief until experience in some form compels it to do so. Being, for example, extremely important to itself, it assumes that it is extremely important to the universe also. The earth is the center of all existing things, man is the child and the protégé of those gods who transcend and who will ultimately enable him to transcend all the evils which he has been compelled to recognize. The world and all that it contains were designed for him, and even those things which seem noxious have their usefulness only temporarily hid. Since he knows but little he is free to imagine, and imagination is always the creature of desire.

II

The world which any consciousness inhabits is a world made up in part of experience and in part of fancy. No experience, and hence no knowledge, is complete, but the gaps which lie between the solid fragments are filled in with shadows. Connections, explanations, and reasons are supplied by the imagination, and thus the world gets its patterned completeness from material which is spun out of the desires. But as time goes on and experience accumulates there remains less and less scope for the fancy. The universe becomes more and more what experience has revealed, less and less what imagination has created, and hence, since it was not designed to suit man's needs, less and less what he would have it be. With increasing knowledge his power to manipulate his physical environment increases, but in gaining the knowledge which enables him to do so he surrenders insensibly the power which in his ignorance he had to mold the universe. The forces of nature obey him, but in learning to master them he has in another sense allowed them to master him. He has exchanged the universe which his desires created, the universe made for man, for the universe of nature of which he is only a part. Like the child growing into manhood, he passes from a world which is fitted to him into a world for which he must fit himself.

If, then, the world of poetry, mythology, and religion represents the world as a man would like to have it, while science represents the world as he gradually comes to discover it, we need only compare the two to realize how irreconcilable they appear. For the cozy bowl of the sky arched in a protecting curve above him he must exchange the cold immensities of space and, for the spiritual order which he has designed, the chaos of nature. God he had loved *because* God was anthropomorphic, because He was made in man's own image, with purposes and desires which were human and hence understandable. But Nature's purpose, if purpose she can be said to have, is no purpose of his and is not understandable in his terms. Her desire merely to live and to propagate in innumerable forms, her ruthless indifference to his values, and the blindness of her irresistible will strike terror to his soul, and he comes in the fullness of his experience to realize that the ends which he proposes to himself—happiness and order and reason—are ends which he must achieve, if he achieve them at all, in her despite. Formerly he had believed in even his darkest moments that the universe was rational if he could only grasp its rationality, but gradually he comes to suspect that rationality is an attribute of himself alone and that there is no reason to suppose that his own life has any more meaning than the life of the humblest insect that crawls from one annihilation to another. Nature, in her blind thirst for life, has filled every possible cranny of the rotting earth with some sort of fantastic creature, and among them man is but one—perhaps the most miserable of all, because he is the only one in whom the instinct of life falters long enough to enable it to ask the question "Why?" As long as life is regarded as having been created, creating may be held to imply a purpose, but merely to have come into being is, in all likelihood, merely to go out of it also.

Fortunately, perhaps, man, like the individual child, was spared in his cradle the knowledge which he could not bear. Illusions have been lost one by one. God, instead of disappearing in an instant, has retreated step by step and surrendered gradually his control of the universe. Once he decreed the fall of every sparrow and counted the hairs upon every head; a little later he became merely the original source of the laws of nature, and even today there are thousands who, unable to bear the thought of losing him completely, still fancy that they can distinguish the uncertain outlines of a misty figure. But the rôle which he plays grows less and less, and man is left more and more alone in a universe to which he is completely alien. His world was once, like the child's world, three-quarters myth and poetry. His teleological concepts molded it into a form which he could appreciate and he gave to it moral laws which would make it meaningful, but step by step the outlines of nature have thrust themselves upon him, and for the dream which he made is substituted a reality devoid of any pattern which he can understand.

In the course of this process innumerable readjustments have been made, and always with the effort to disturb as little as possible the myth which is so much more full of human values than the fact which comes in some measure to replace it. Thus, for example, the Copernican theory of astronomy, removing the earth from the center of the universe and assigning it a very insignificant place among an infinitude of whirling motes, was not merely resisted as a fact but was, when finally accepted, accepted as far as possible without its implications. Even if taken entirely by itself and without the whole system of facts of which it is a part, it renders extremely improbable the assumption, fundamental in most human thought, that the universe has man as its center and is hence understandable in his terms, but this implication was disregarded just as, a little later, the implications of the theory of evolution were similarly disregarded. It is not likely that if man had been aware from the very beginning that his world was a mere detail in the universe, and himself merely one of the innumerable species of living things, he would ever have come to think of himself, as he even now tends to do, as a being whose desires must be somehow satisfiable and whose reason must be matched by some similar reason in nature. But the myth, having been once established, persists long after the assumptions upon which it was made have been destroyed, because, being born of desire, it is far more satisfactory than any fact.

Unfortunately, perhaps, experience does not grow at a constant, but at an accelerated, rate. The Greeks who sought knowledge, not through the study of nature but through the examination of their own minds, developed a philosophy which was really analogous to myth, because the laws which determined its growth were dictated by human desires and they discovered few facts capable of disturbing the pattern which they devised. The Middle Ages retreated still further into themselves, but with the Renaissance man began to surrender himself to nature, and the sciences, each nourishing the other, began their iconoclastic march. Three centuries lay between the promulgation of the Copernican theory and the publication of the *Origin of Species,* but in sixty-odd years which have elapsed since that latter event the blows have fallen with a rapidity which left no interval for recovery. The structures which are variously known as mythology, religion, and philosophy, and which are alike in that each has as its function the interpretation of experience in terms which have human values, have collapsed under the force of successive attacks and shown themselves utterly incapable of assimilating the new stores of experience which have been dumped upon the world. With increasing completeness science maps out the pattern of nature, but the latter has no relation to the pattern of human needs and feelings.

Consider, for example, the plight of ethics. Historical criticism having destroyed what used to be called by people of learning and intelligence "Christian Evidences," and biology having shown how unlikely it is that man is the recipient of any transcendental knowledge, there remains no foundation in authority for ideas of right and wrong; and if, on the other hand, we turn to the traditions of the human race anthropology is ready to prove that no consistent human tradition has ever existed. Custom has furnished the only basis which ethics have ever had, and there is no conceivable human action which custom has not at one time justified and at another condemned. Standards are imaginary things, and yet it is extremely doubtful if man can live well, either spiritually or physically, without the belief that they are somehow real. Without them society lapses into anarchy and the individual becomes aware of an intolerable disharmony between himself and the universe. Instinctively and emotionally he is an ethical animal. No known race is so low in the scale of civilization that it has not attributed a moral order to the world, because no known race is so little human as not to suppose a moral order so innately desirable as to have an inevitable existence. It is man's most fundamental myth, and life seems meaningless to him without it. Yet, as that systematized and cululative experience which is called science displaces one after another the myths which have been generated by need, it grows more and more likely that he must remain an ethical animal in a universe which contains no ethical element.

III

Mystical philosophers have sometimes said that they "accepted the universe." They have, that is to say, formed of it some conception which answered the emotional needs of their spirit and which brought them a sense of being in harmony with its aims and processes. They have been aware of no needs which Nature did not seem to supply and of no ideals which she too did not seem to recognize. They have felt themselves one with her because they have had the strength of imagination to make her over in their own image, and it is doubtful if any man can live at peace who does not thus feel himself at home. But as the world assumes the shape which science gives it, it becomes more and more difficult to find such emotional correspondences. Whole realms of human feeling, like the realm of ethics, find no place for themselves in the pattern of nature and generate needs for which no satisfaction is supplied. What man knows is everywhere at war with what he wants.

In the course of a few centuries his knowledge, and hence the universe of which he finds himself an inhabitant, has been completely revolutionized, but his instincts and his emotions have remained, relatively at least, unchanged. He is still, as he always was, adjusted to the orderly, purposeful, humanized world which all peoples unburdened by experience have figured to themselves, but that world no longer exists. He has the same sense of dignity to which the myth of his descent from the gods was designed to minister, and the same innate purposefulness which led him to attribute a purpose to nature, but he can no longer think in terms appropriate to either. The world which his reason and his investigation reveal is a world which his emotions cannot comprehend.

Casually he accepts the spiritual iconoclasm of science, and in the detachment of everyday life he learns to play with the cynical wisdom of biology and psychology, which explain away the awe of emotional experience just as earlier science explained away the awe of conventional piety. Yet, under the stress of emotional crises, knowledge is quite incapable of controlling his emotions or of justifying them to himself. In love, he calls upon the illusions of man's grandeur and dignity to help him accept his emotions, and faced with tragedy he calls upon illusion to dignify his suffering; but lyric flight is checked by the rationality which he has cultivated, and in the world of metabolism and hormones, repressions and complexes, he finds no answer for his needs. He is feeling about love, for example, much as the troubadour felt, but he thinks about it in a very different way. Try as he may, the two halves of his soul can hardly be made to coalesce, and he cannot either feel as his intelligence tells him that he should feel or think as his emotions would have him think, and thus he is reduced to mocking his torn and divided soul. In the grip of passion he cannot, as some romanticist might have done, accept it with a religious trust in the mystery of love, nor yet can he regard it as a psychiatrist, himself quite free from emotion, might suggest—merely as an interesting specimen of psychical botany. Man *qua* thinker may delight in the intricacies of psychology, but man *qua* lover has not learned to feel in its terms; so that, though complexes and ductless glands may serve to explain the feelings of another, one's own still demand all those symbols of the ineffable in which one has long ceased to believe.

Time was when the scientist, the poet, and the philosopher walked hand in hand. In the universe which the one perceived the other found himself comfortably at home. But the world of modern science is one in which the intellect alone can rejoice. The mind leaps, and leaps perhaps with a sort of elation, through the immensities of space, but the spirit, frightened and cold, longs to have once more above its head the inverted bowl beyond which may lie whatever paradise its desires may create. The lover who surrendered himself to the Implacable Aphrodite or who fancied his foot upon the lowest rung of the Platonic ladder of love might retain his self-respect, but one can neither resist nor yield gracefully to a carefully catalogued psychosis. A happy life is a sort of poem, with a poem's elevation and dignity, but emotions cannot be dignified unless they are first respected. They must seem to correspond with, to be justified by, something in the structure of the universe itself; but though it was the function of religion and philosophy to hypostatize some such correspondence, to project a humanity upon nature, or at least to conceive of a humane force above and beyond her, science finds no justification for such a process and is content instead to show how illusions were born.

The most ardent love of truth, the most resolute determination to follow nature no matter to what black abyss she may lead, need not blind one to the fact that many of the lost illusions had, to speak the language of science, a survival value. Either individuals or societies whose life is imbued with a cheerful certitude, whose aims are clear, and whose sense of the essential rightness of life is strong, live and struggle with an energy unknown to the skeptical and the pessimistic. Whatever the limitations of their intellects as instruments of criticism, they possess the physical and emotional vigor which is, unlike critical intelligence, analogous to the processes of nature. They found empires and conquer wildernesses, and they pour the excess of their energy into works of art which the intelligence of more sophisticated peoples continues to admire even though it has lost the faith in life which is requisite for the building of a Chartres or the carving of a Venus de Milo. The one was not erected to a law of nature or the other designed to celebrate the libido, for each presupposed a sense of human dignity which science nowhere supports.

Thus man seems caught in a dilemma which his intellect has devised. Any deliberately managed return to a state of relative ignorance, however desirable it might be argued to be, is obviously out of the question. We cannot, as the naïve proponents of the various religions, new and old, seem to assume, believe one thing and forget another merely because we happen to be convinced that it would be desirable to do so; and it is worth observing that the new psychology, with its penetrating analysis of the influence of desire upon belief, has so adequately warned the reason of the tricks which the will can play upon it that it has greatly decreased the possibility of beneficent delusion and serves to hold the mind in a steady contemplation of that from which it would fain escape. Weak and uninstructed intelligences take refuge in the monotonous repetition of once living creeds, or are even reduced to the desperate expedient of going to sleep amid the formulae of the flabby pseudo-religions in which the modern world is so prolific. But neither of these classes affords any aid to the robust but serious mind which is searching for some terms upon which it may live.

And if we are, as by this time we should be, free

from any teleological delusion, if we no longer make the unwarranted assumption that every human problem is somehow of necessity solvable, we must confess it may be that for the sort of being whom we have described no survival is possible in any form like that which his soul has now taken. He is a fantastic thing that has developed sensibilities and established values beyond the nature which gave him birth. He is of all living creatures the one to whom the earth is the least satisfactory. He has arrived at a point where he can no longer delude himself as to the extent of his predicament, and should he either become modified or disappear the earth would continue to spin and the grass to grow as it has always done. Of the thousands of living species the vast majority would be as unaware of his passing as they are unaware now of his presence, and he would go as a shadow goes. His arts, his religions, and his civilizations—these are fair and wonderful things, but they are fair and wonderful to him alone. With the extinction of his poetry would come also the extinction of the only sensibility for which it has any meaning, and there would remain nothing capable of feeling a loss. Nothing would be left to label the memory of his discontent "divine," and those creatures who find in nature no lack would resume their undisputed possession of the earth.

Anthropoid in form some of them might continue to be, and possessed as well of all of the human brain that makes possible a cunning adaptation to the conditions of physical life. To them nature might yield up subtler secrets than any yet penetrated; their machines might be more wonderful and their bodies more healthy than any yet known—even though there had passed away, not merely all myth and poetry, but the need for them as well. Cured of his transcendental cravings, content with things as they are, accepting the universe as experience had shown it to be, man would be freed of his soul and, like the other animals, either content or at least desirous of nothing which he might not hope ultimately to obtain.

Nor can it be denied that certain adumbrations of this type have before now come into being. Among those of keener intellect there are scientists to whom the test tube and its contents are all-sufficient, and among those of coarser grain, captains of finance and builders of mills, there are those to whom the acquirement of wealth and power seems to constitute a life in which no lack can be perceived. Doubtless they are not new types; doubtless they have always existed; but may they not be the strain from which Nature will select the coming race? Is not their creed the creed of Nature, and are they not bound to triumph over those whose illusions are no longer potent because they are no longer really believed? Certain philosophers, clinging desperately to the ideal of a humanized world, have proposed a retreat into the imagination. Bertrand Russell in his popular essay, *A Free Man's Worship*, Unamuno and Santayana *passim* throughout their works, have argued that the way of salvation lay in a sort of ironic belief, in a determination to act as though one still believed the things which once were really held true. But is not this a desperate expedient, a last refuge likely to appeal only to the leaders of a lost cause? Does it not represent the last, least substantial, phase of fading faith, something which borrows what little substance it seems to have from a reality of the past? If it seems half real to the sons of those who lived in the spiritual world of which it is a shadow, will it not seem, a little further removed, only a faint futility? Surely it has but little to oppose to those who come armed with the certitudes of science and united with, not fleeing from, the nature amid which they live.

And if the dilemma here described is itself a delusion it is at least as vividly present and as terribly potent as those other delusions which have shaped or deformed the human spirit. There is no significant contemporary writer upon philosophy, ethics, or aesthetics whose speculations do not lead him to it in one form or another, and even the less reflective are aware of it in their own way. Both our practical morality and our emotional lives are adjusted to a world which no longer exists. In so far as we adhere to a code of conduct, we do so largely because certain habits still persist, not because we can give any logical reason for preferring them, and in so far as we indulge ourselves in the primitive emotional satisfactions—romantic love, patriotism, zeal for justice, and so forth—our satisfaction is the result merely of the temporary suspension of our disbelief in the mythology upon which they are founded. Traditionalists in religion are fond of asserting that our moral codes are flimsy because they are rootless; but, true as this is, it is perhaps not so important as the fact that our emotional lives are rootless too.

If the gloomy vision of a dehumanized world which has just been evoked is not to become a reality, some complete readjustment must be made, and at least two generations have found themselves unequal to the task. The generation of Thomas Henry Huxley, so busy with destruction as never adequately to realize how much it was destroying, fought with such zeal against frightened conservatives that it never took time to do more than assert with some vehemence that all would be well, and the generation that followed either danced amid the ruins or sought by various compromises to save the remains of a few tottering structures. But neither patches nor evasions will serve. It is not a changed world but a new one in which man must henceforth live if he lives at all, for all his premises have been destroyed and he must proceed to new conclusions. The values which he thought established have been swept away along with the rules by which he thought they might be attained.

To this fact many are not yet awake, but our novels, our poems, and our pictures are enough to reveal that a generation aware of its predicament is at hand. It has awakened to the fact that both the ends which its fathers proposed to themselves and the emotions from which they drew their strength seem irrelevant and remote. With a smile, sad or mocking, according to individual temperament, it regards those works of the past in which were summed up the values of life. The romantic ideal of a world well lost for love and the classic ideal of austere dignity seem equally ridiculous, equally meaningless when referred, not to the temper of the past, but to the temper of the present. The passions which swept through the once major poets no longer awaken any profound response, and only in the bleak, tortuous complexities of a T. S. Eliot does it find its moods given adequate expression. Here disgust speaks with a robust voice and denunciation is confident, but ecstasy, flickering and uncertain, leaps fitfully up only to sink back among the cinders. And if the poet, with his gift of keen perceptions and his power of organization, can achieve only the most momentary and unstable adjustments, what hope can there be for those whose spirit is a less powerful instrument?

And yet it is with such as he, baffled, but content with nothing which plays only upon the surface, that the hope for a still humanized future must rest. No one can tell how many of the old values must go or how new the new will be. Thus, while under the influence of the old mythology the sexual instinct was transformed into romantic love and tribal solidarity into the religion of patriotism, there is nothing in the modern consciousness capable of effecting these transmutations. Neither the one nor the other is capable of being, as it once was, the *raison d'être* of a life or the motif of a poem which is not, strictly speaking, derivative and anachronistic. Each is fading, each becoming as much a shadow as devotion to the cult of purification through self-torture. Either the instincts upon which they are founded will achieve new transformations or they will remain merely instincts, regarded as having no particular emotional significance in a spiritual world which, if it exists at all, will be as different from the spiritual world of, let us say, Robert Browning as that world is different from the world of Cato the Censor.

As for this present unhappy time, haunted by ghosts from a dead world and not yet at home in its own, its predicament is not, to return to the comparison with which we began, unlike the predicament of the adolescent who has not yet learned to orient himself without reference to the mythology amid which his childhood was passed. He still seeks in the world of his experience for the values which he had found there, and he is aware only of a vast disharmony. But boys—most of them, at least—grow up, and the world of adult consciousness has always held a relation to myth intimate enough to make readjustment possible. The finest spirits have bridged the gulf, have carried over with them something of a child's faith, and only the coarsest have grown into something which was no more than finished animality. Today the gulf is broader, the adjustment more difficult, than ever it was before, and even the possibility of an actual human maturity is problematic. There impends for the human spirit either extinction or a readjustment more stupendous than any made before.

The Paradox of Humanism

Words which are spelled with a capital letter are peculiarly dangerous to thought. One commonly uses them to designate a complex of ideas which has never been adequately analyzed, and their meaning varies from age to age as well as from person to person. A whole volume might profitably be devoted to trace, for example, the history of the various senses in which the term "Nature" has been employed, and in a chapter of his *Reconstruction in Philosophy* John Dewey has, indeed, sketched the outline of a part of such a volume. He has shown how the eighteenth century habitually employed it in reference to a closed system of logical ideas, and how it referred thereby to a hypothetical order of values which has no connection whatever with the nature which it is the scientist's business to investigate. Dewey might have gone on to inquire by what confusion the contemporaries of Mozart were led to praise as "natural" musical compositions as elaborately formal as his, and by what perversion the same adjective was used to praise the strained artificial romanticism of Kotzebue's lugubrious dramas. But at least he carries the analysis far enough for his own purpose as well for ours, which is merely to illustrate how dangerous it is to use such a word without a most exacting investigation of its content.

In the present instance we are to be concerned with another capitalized word, "Humanism," a word which has undergone similar variations of meaning; which has been used in similarly opposed senses; and which, like "Nature," has been most frequently employed rather because of certain affective connotations than because of any exact meaning. The Renaissance scholars who introduced it did so in order to define a culture which was not theological, and the contrast chiefly implied was a contrast between that which is human and that which is divine. The modern use of the term arose, on the other hand, as a result of the theory of evolution, and it is chiefly employed by those who feel some temperamental repugnance to the nineteenth century's tendency to study man chiefly as a form of animal life. It has managed, moreover, to get itself confused with semireligious protests against the radical tendencies of contemporary society, and so vague has it become that, if we are to talk of humanism and its paradox, we must define our term.

But if "human" and the words formed from it can have an exact meaning, as distinguished from the vague connotation of a complex of ideas and attitudes, that meaning must refer to those qualities, characteristics, and powers which distinguish the human being from the rest of animate nature and which, if they exist, justify us in making a distinction between Man and Nature, even though we are naturalistic enough in our thought to agree that what we really mean is no more than a distinction between man and the rest of nature. It is in that sense that it will be here employed, and the purpose of this chapter is to investigate some of these distinctions and to comment upon the problems which they present to those who are concerned with the potentialities of life. It will arrive at conclusions somewhat at variance with those upon which both the expansive optimistic naturalist and the cautious exponent of dualistic humanism base their respective conceptions of the art of life.

First of all we must be careful to give to the beasts their due, for your self-styled humanist has a churlish habit of calling the most characteristic human vices "animal." In particular he is inclined to describe any sexual indulgence of which he does not approve as "bestial," and more especially still to say of a man or woman who makes the pleasures of sense the chief business of life that he is yielding to his "animal nature." But while such a description may serve a useful homiletic purpose, and while it may, since man is by nature proud of his humanity and anxious to distinguish himself from his humbler cousins, sometimes incline him to struggle against tendencies thus cavalierly labeled, it can hardly satisfy the philosopher, who will recognize its injustice.

A century and a half ago man was first described as the only animal who loves all the year around, and in general the distinction will still hold. Not only is it true that the animals rigidly subordinate sex to the function of reproduction, but it is also, according to anthropologists, notoriously true that the more primitive races of men closely resemble animals in this respect. Early superficial observers who watched the rites with which savages celebrate the act of physical union and who noted the elaborate sexual symbolism which runs through certain of their dances leaped to the conclusion that they were obsessed with sexual ideas and labeled them "obscene." But a more intimate investigation of primitive society and the primitive mind has reversed this idea. In comparison with civilized man the savage is, like the animal, what we should be tempted to call singularly sexless. His mind does not turn readily or habitually in that direction; his passions require an extraordinary amount of stimulation before they are aroused; and his "obscene" dances are not the result of fantastic corruption but are, on the contrary, necessary to stimulate in him a sufficient interest in the sexual functions adequately to reproduce his kind. The Don Juan, on the other hand, is characteristically human, and complexly human at that. Neither the animal nor the primitive man could "live for love" in the physical sense, although both, as will be indicated later, can realize more perfectly perhaps than civilized man that selflessness which is sometimes also called love and which is not infrequently spoken of as the highest achievement of the human spirit.

Chastity is not, then, human in the sense in which we have defined the term. To man and to man alone belong both that exaggeration of the sexual impulse which makes it possible, in certain cases, for him to subordinate everything else to it, and also that unfortunate disharmony which leads him, in other cases, to devote his chief attention to maintaining and celebrating his resistance to similar impulses. But chastity, in the sense of an inherent tendency to avoid an absorption in the sexual instinct, is rather animal than human. And if, then, debauchery rather than abstinence is "humanistic" we may proceed to examine certain of the other virtues, and we need not be too much surprised if we find that many are, at best, not part of that which particularly distinguishes man from the rest of nature.

Certainly paternal or maternal love is nowhere more perfectly illustrated than among the animals. A devotion to the welfare of children, a complete absorption in the business of parenthood, and a willingness not only to subordinate all other interests to those of the offspring but, if necessary, to lay down life itself upon the altar of family duty—such devotion, which, in the case of human beings, would be celebrated as an unusual and shining example of the heights to which human nature can on rare occasions rise, is a common occurrence among animals and it is not the occasion

of any special wonder. But on the other hand that un-
willingness on the part of the parent to subordinate
himself entirely to the welfare of his children, that
tendency to go on "living one's own life" which certain "humanists" denounce as the result of "naturalistic" literature and thought, is, on the contrary, quite distinctly human. Our kind has, in addition, developed
that particular perversion which sometimes leads
mothers or fathers selfishly to indulge the luxury of
their parental emotions to a harmful degree and to
pursue their grown children with a fatal solicitude of
which no animal would be capable; but devotion
which perfectly fulfills its function is—shall we say—
"bestial."

It is hardly necessary to pursue this painful inquiry
further, but in general it may be remarked that those
virtues whose tendency it is to promote the welfare
of the species without regard to the welfare of the individual, and which result in the complete subordina-
tion of any real or fancied "self-realization," are conspicuously animal, while the revolt against them is
distinctly human. Even the more complex social
virtues grow from roots which may be traced in animal nature more readily than the roots of many
human vices; and, since it is upon the social virtues
that the modern humanist lays greatest stress, it would
be more appropriate for him to call himself by some
name which would suggest that the fear lying behind
his protestations is in reality a fear lest man should become too exclusively "human" and lest, detaching himself too completely from animal tendencies, he should
become no longer willing to live in a fashion that
would make possible the continuity of society.

Perhaps, on the other hand, the inclusive term "individualism" is the one which will best describe the
attitude toward living which is most characteristically
human. The animal, absorbed as he is in the business
of arranging for the survival of himself and his kind,

seems far less capable than man of distinguishing between himself and his race. We need not naïvely attribute to him any philosophy in order to explain his
behavior, but it is evident that he *acts* as though he
had arrived at that attitude which is accounted by
some exponents of social ethics as the ultimate human
ideal, and which consists in an identification with society so close as to make meaningless any distinction
between private and public good. He does not ask what
he gets out of life, nor why he should sacrifice himself
in the laborious business of continuing it. The lair or
the nest is prepared, and the young are born. They are
nourished, defended, given such education as they
need, and then, when the time comes, the parents die
quietly, quite as though they were as completely aware
as Mr. Shaw's Ancients that the important thing is,
not that any individual should have arrived at any "fulfillment" of his own, but that life should go on. Yet,
though something of this kind has been often enough
described as the highest human virtue, the human being seems incapable of consciously achieving what the
animal possesses as part of his natural endowment.

Doubtless the more primitive races come nearest to
it, and in civilized communities it is the simplest people who, at least according to the literature of whole-
some sentiment, most conspicuously exhibit this willingness to refrain from any demand that life should
justify itself in their own persons by being worth
while to them as individuals, and who are therefore
most perfect in the social virtues. But even among
those who acquiesce most patiently in the burdens of
life there are usually moments of analysis and rebellion. "Quiet desperation," that famous phrase which
Thoreau used to describe the mood of the average man,
is the result of an impotent protest against the realization that he is playing the animal's part without being
blessed with the animal's unconscious acquiescence;
and the more highly developed the reflective powers of

the individual become, the more likely is that quiet desperation to become an active rebellion which expresses itself in self-regarding vices.

The fact that the belief in immortality is practically coextensive with the human race does not, unfortunately, prove that the belief is well founded, but it does prove that the desire for a life beyond this life is universal, and that, in turn, may be used to show that individualism is one of the most fundamental human traits, since the desire for immortality is an expression of the human protest against the scheme of nature which takes so little account of man and his demands. When first he dimly perceives that his chief function is merely to see that others like himself shall carry life on after he has had his busy and futile hour of consciousness, he, as an individual, revolts against the natural order, and in imagination he projects himself forward into another existence in which that consciousness, so he assures himself, shall continue to exist. He is no longer willing, as the animal is, to accept the fate which makes him only a part of something larger than himself, and thus religion, in so far as it is essentially a belief in immortality, is merely the first stage in the process by which man detaches himself from Nature, asserts the importance of himself as an individual, and proposes to himself ends and values which do not exist for her.

And if the belief in immortality be so regarded, its chief function will appear to depend upon the power which it has of enabling the human being to continue in the practice of the animal virtues. The heightened consciousness which makes him aware of himself as an individual leads him to demand some adequate motive which will take the place of the instinct which is by itself sufficient for the beast. In him the will to live is not so nearly unconditional, and neither does it discriminate so little between individual and racial survival. But by promising himself an eternal life he achieves a conscious substitute for the animal's unconscious concern for the species, and by associating the animal virtues with his eternal welfare he obtains a motive for their practice.

Hence it is that those for whom the belief in immortality is most vivid are the most likely to practice the virtues which have a survival value and the least likely to deviate into either those virtues or those vices which are exclusively human. But, as skepticism grows, the pattern of human conduct inevitably changes. The demand that life justify itself can no longer be postponed, and hence there begins the search for values which shall have meaning for the individual consciousness as opposed to those which have meaning only for Nature and her inscrutable appetite for mere life in itself. The simpler man, caught in a meaningless but exacting round of duties, does no more than fall into that "quiet desperation" which we must again thank Thoreau for having so exactly named. Probably he comforts himself with some vague dream concerning some future fulfillment on the part of his children, and he does not dare to realize that their happiness will be, at best, as shadowy as his —that it too will consist in a projection forward upon still another generation, and that his children too will receive his own illusory sense of achievement when they have in reality done no more than pass the problem on to fresh bodies which are doomed to the same futile exhaustion. But minds which are keener and wills which are stronger than the average do not rest in "quiet desperation" palliated by illusion. They demand of life some meaning comprehensible to them, and they set themselves up against Nature because they have come to realize that her values are not for them and her contentment not theirs.

Thus even the Don Juan is characteristically human, because he has seized upon something which Nature has instituted for her purposes and has tried to utilize it for his own. However dangerous he may be to society, and however great his own failure may ultimately seem even, perhaps, to himself, his effort is the type of all purely human effort because it is essentially an attempt to make some process of life significant and valuable in itself; and it is doubtless the fact that he presents so readily comprehensible a symbol of the humanizing process which has made him so eternally popular in imaginative literature. Yet, however easily understandable his effort may be from a human standpoint, it will serve to illustrate most strikingly how this standpoint may be diametrically opposed to that of Nature, upon whom, nevertheless, even man must depend for the health of his own body and the welfare of his race. The Don Juan may find himself comprehended and pardoned by his fellow men, but Nature takes no account of even the most reasonable of human excuses.

III

To those who study her, this Nature reveals herself as extraordinarily fertile and ingenious in devising *means,* but she has no *ends* which the human mind has been able to discover or comprehend. Perhaps, indeed, the very conception of an end or ultimate purpose is exclusively human; but at least it must be said that the most characteristically human effort is that to transform a means into an end, and that it is such an effort which explains the Don Juan, as well as the more complex forms assumed by that curiously modified animal which is described as human. The artist and the philosopher have been generally recognized as representing the most highly developed type of that intelligence which we admire as something beyond mere animal instinct or animal cunning, but the concern of both is not with the *means* of Nature but with the *ends* of man. By thought the philosopher attempts to discover what these may be, and the artist, who is thus closely parallel to the Don Juan, attempts to achieve them by arresting the attention upon certain moments in life and proclaiming that it is for them as ends in themselves that life exists.

Yet the plain man has always, and not without reason, distrusted the philosopher and the artist. Observation has taught him that the latter, especially, is likely to be too ferociously intent upon his own ends to be other than a bad father and an unreliable citizen; and more obscurely he realizes that, even when this cannot be specifically charged, both are too detached from animal impulses to carry on the business of survival and propagation with that single-minded intensity which has populated every cranny of the earth. Nor can the philosopher or the artist himself fail to recognize the justice of this distrust. At one moment he might be inclined to suppose the evolution of humanity to be in his direction, but at the next he is compelled to realize that a world of philosophers and artists is unthinkable. The foundations of the society in which he exists were built up and are sustained by people who were active in a way in which he can never be. He is not, in the most fundamental or necessary sense, useful or productive; he is parasitic upon a society which depends upon those endowed with an unquestioning animal vigor, and without them he could not exist. A decadent society, he realizes, is merely one in which too large a proportion of the population is concerned with "ends" and with self-realization. While some pursue pleasure and end in debauchery, the others create works of art or lose themselves in speculation concerning the elusive *summum bonum,* but too few are left to sustain the natural substructure with that energy which is drawn from instinct alone. While the bush blossoms all too profusely, the roots die away, and before long the whole organism is dead. And thus the artist-philosopher, who, correctly enough, considers himself as the most exclusively human of human beings, is left in a dilemma, for he is compelled to recognize humanism as the ultimate enemy of those natural impulses which have made the human animal possible.

Sensibility and intelligence arose in the animal in order to serve animal purposes, for through the first it was able to distinguish those things which favor the survival of it and its race and through the second it was able to go about in a more efficient manner to secure them. Both were, like all things in nature, merely means toward the achievement of that humanly incomprehensible end, mere survival; but the philosopher-artist has detached both from their natural places as mere devices, and in attempting to make each an end in itself he has discovered that when they are so detached they are capable of becoming impediments to the attainment of the superhuman aims they were developed to promote. When sensibility has been detached from its animal setting it may, in its crudest form, become the erotomania of the Don Juan, or, in a more exalted form, it may develop into a quest for that self-justifying Beauty which is humanly valuable but biologically useless and which it is the artist's chief effort to capture; when intelligence is detached, it not only tends to paralyze natural impulse by criticizing natural aims but develops certain intellectual virtues which are biologic vices. We are, for example, inclined to regard skepticism, irony, and above all the power of dispassionate analysis as the marks of the most distinctly human intelligence. We admire the man whose reason is capable of more than scheming, whose logic is not the mere rationalization of his desires, and who can follow through an argument to its conclusion even though that conclusion is not one favorable to himself, his party, his country, or his species. But intelligence as detached as this is a vital liability. It puts the man or the race which possesses it at a disadvantage in dealing with those whose intelligence faithfully serves their purpose by enabling them to scheme for their ends and to justify to themselves their desires. Such is the animal function of intelligence, and whenever it develops beyond this it is useful for contemplation and it has a beauty of its own, but it is only humanly valuable and it inhibits rather than aids that effective action in the pursuit of natural ends which was the original function of mind.

And incidentally it may be remarked that the dilemma here indicated is the largest aspect of the one which in a more immediately insistent way pins between its horns every nation which has developed a national mind capable of detachment. Thanks to this mind, the nation is compelled to criticize that naïve patriotism which leads every race to regard itself as evidently superior to every other; it hesitates to embark upon a career of imperialism and to subject the surrounding people to its dominion because it has passed beyond that stage of invigorating delusion which could make it fancy itself master by right of an inherent superiority; and it sees both sides. And yet it must purchase this intellectual and moral superiority at the price of a gradual decline, and it is well that it should do so in a full consciousness of the price. One after another the great nations of history have founded upon aggression the civilization which then supported for a time, but for a time only, great periods of human culture which flourished at their height just as the substructure crumbled. Animals made men possible and conquerors prepared the way for poets and philosophers, but neither poet nor philosopher can survive long after he has parted company with his progenitor and opponent.

Nor need we be surprised to see races enfeebled by civilization as though by disease, for the distinction between the vices and the virtues of the complexly organized man is a human, not a natural, distinction, and the two develop together as he humanizes himself. That detachment of mind from its function which makes philosophy possible and which encourages dispassionate analysis is exactly parallel to the detachment of the sexual functions from their purposes which results in the cult of the senses. Thought for thought's sake is a kind of perversion whose essential character is not changed because it happens to illustrate the fact that human virtues may be biologic vices, and there is no reason to suppose that from a strictly biological standpoint one detachment is not as bad as the other. Civilizations die from philosophical calm, irony, and the sense of fair play quite as surely as they die of debauchery.

IV

Whatever we may think of the recurrent "live dangerously" of Nietzsche's various testaments, the injunction is one which in certain spiritual senses we cannot choose but obey, for, the higher the mental organization which men achieve, the more precariously is it poised. The simple automatic responses of the amoeba serve it with dependable regularity. It may die a physical death, but it may neither lose its mind nor sink to depths of moral degradation; and what is true of the amoeba is so largely true throughout the whole range of animal life that the difference between it and the highest ape is not in that respect so great as the difference between the ape and man. Consciousness, understanding, and the powers of judgment and choice, even though these may be, as the behavioristic psychologists maintain, only a sort of illusion, are accompanied by capacities for ghastly failure unknown to the animal. To live humanly is, in that sense, to live dangerously; and the more completely human we are, the less our motives, our impulses, and our values are those which we have in common with the other animals, the more dangerous our lives come perforce to be.

To renounce Nature and natural ends, to go even so far as to find them insufficient, is to renounce at the same time the sure guidance which she gives to those who are content to accept it without question. Upon ourselves we impose both the task of conceiving ends independent of hers and the task of devising means to attain them. Equipped with certain capacities capable of certain developments, we pervert them from their uses, and we suffer as a result from a permanent maladjustment. Both mind and body are subject to abuses, and both are thereby corrupted. Even when our efforts are momentarily successful, even when some great man or some resplendent civilization seems to justify the effort to transcend nature, the equilibrium achieved is an unstable one. The great mind and the great culture are alike poised over an abyss and are in perpetual danger of tumbling headlong. Civilization has been called a dance, but the feet of the dancers do not rest upon terra firma. It is danced upon a tight rope that sways in the breeze. The nerves and muscles of the performers are tense. They wave reckless defiance to the force of gravity, but they are in truth ill equipped for the airy stunt. Their feet are designed to rest upon the earth; it is even at the expense of a certain strain upon their bodies that they walk upright rather than upon all fours, and their balance is far from sure.

The ant who crawls unnoticed in the grass below is much older than they, and in the eyes of Nature he has made a much greater success in life. Long before they felt the first stirrings of proud superiority he was fixed in wise habits that have never varied. For thousands of years his frozen perfection has endured and, if he has no art and no philosophy, he is perfect in social virtue. He has merged his own interests completely with those of his kind, and he makes no demands for himself which will interfere with the prosperity of the colony which he inhabits.

His industry and his foresight have always been admired, but only patient observation has revealed how much more complex his virtues are. Not only does he perform without question the part assigned him in the division of labor, but he has even achieved a control over the processes of reproduction which enables him to see to it that just the right number of each type of citizen shall be born; and, far from allowing himself to be disturbed by the distractions of love, he has consented, in the interests of efficiency, to remain sexless, while certain specialists are endowed with powers of reproduction. He is not primitive or simple, but he has let Nature have her way with him and she has rewarded him with a peaceful security which her more rebellious children can never hope to obtain.

But when a man looks at an ant he realizes the meaning of his humanity. If he happens to be one of those whose thought has concerned itself much with sociology he may be struck by the fact that the anthill represents something very close to that communistic Utopia generally evolved by the imagination which busies itself with picturing an ideal society, and yet the contemplation of this realized and eternal perfection strikes a chill to his heart, because it seems to have no meaning or value and because he perceives that, so far as he is concerned, Nature's masterpiece might be destroyed without causing him to feel that anything valuable had passed away.

This perfected society is, that is to say, utterly devoid of human values, and its perfection is made possible by that very fact. It owes both its stability and its efficient harmony to the absence of any tendency on the part of individuals either to question the value of existence or to demand anything for themselves. Students of its evolution tell us that the automatic and yet cunning elaborateness of the life-habits which it reveals are explainable only on the theory that insects were once more variable, perhaps we can say more "intelligent," than they are now, but that, as perfection of adjustment was reached, habit became all-sufficient, and hence the biologically useless consciousness faded away until they are probably now not aware of their actions in any fashion analogous to the awareness of the mammals who are in certain respects so much less perfect than they.

And yet who, however weary he may be of human instability and discontent and violence, would exchange his state for that of the ant? However much he may admire the social virtues and however much he may be repelled by the selfish disorder of modern individualistic society, he must realize that whatever gives to life the qualities which make him cling to it resides somewhere in that region whence spring the protests which make the regularity and peace of the anthill impossible for man. Complete non-being seems to him scarcely less ghastly than the automatic existence which its citizens lead, and so it is ultimately to the biologic vices of the human being that he clings.

It is through these latter that he suffers, and through them that he, as an animal, fails. They are the source of the *taedium vitae* which oppresses him when he realizes that he is leading a purely natural life and accomplishing only natural aims; they inspire him also to those rebellions which are impotent because they bring him face to face with the limitations he cannot transcend; and they exact as the penalty of indulgence the ills of mind or flesh which oppress the wearied brain of the thinker or the exhausted body of the debauchee. Yet they constitute his humanity, and it is only as a human being that he cares to live.

v

It would appear, then, that that complex of ideas and preferences which passes current under the name of

humanism may be separated into two distinct parts.
The complex includes on the one hand a tendency to
stress the importance of the social virtues set up in opposition to the destructive, anarchistic tendencies of
what it mistakenly calls the "natural" man, and it includes on the other hand a sympathy with the attempt
to create human, as opposed to natural, values. Yet
these social virtues are, as we have seen, themselves
animal, and among men they flourish most in those
societies where the genuinely human tendencies—both
virtuous and vicious—are least prominent. "Humanism" in this popular sense is thus obviously at war
with itself, for the simple reason that the closer it
comes to a realization of one half its ideal the further
it is bound to be from the possibility of achieving the
other, since the second demands a detachment from
the aims of nature and the first a harmony with them.

The virtues of the half-legendary Spartans will
stand as a fitting symbol of the more austere half of
the idea. The Spartan commonwealth, if we may
trust the image of it which has exercised a continuous
fascination on the imagination of mankind for the very
reason that it does serve as a symbol, was not unlike a
community of insects. It was marked by the discipline,
the regularity, and the patriotism of the anthill. It sub-
ordinated the individual to the state, and it regarded
posterity as the chief of that state's concerns. But it
was thus a "natural" society and it maintained its un-
corrupted animality by a stern contempt for the
virtues as well as the vices which together constituted
the humanism of its great neighbor. A little later
"Roman virtue" looked with a perfectly justified sus-
picion upon Athenian culture, and the Catos were
shrewd enough to perceive what most moderns do not
dare to admit: namely, that a choice must ultimately
be made between a stable, essentially animal existence
and the dangerous—ultimately fatal—life of the society
which starts out in pursuit of purely human values.

Historians looking back upon the rise and fall of civilization have always been perplexed by the fact that societies are most admirable just before they collapse. They have been embarrassed by the necessity of interrupting the description of every golden age in order to point a warning finger at the signs of decay which have a way of manifesting themselves just at the moment when perfection seems about to be reached. To escape from a dilemma they have assumed that the association so often noted between the flowering of the intellect and the decline of national vigor is merely fortuitous, but it may very well be that it is instead the inevitable result of that detachment from nature which we have been describing and which is at once the condition of human greatness and the destruction of animal health.

The antithesis between human and natural ends is thus ultimately irreconcilable, and the most that man can hope for is a recurrent defiance recurrently subdued. He can deviate so far but no further from the animal norm. He can make himself into an artist or a philosopher, but there are limits set both to the perfection of those types and to the extent to which the bulk of any population can be allowed to approach either, for individuals and races alike fall victim to their humanity. In the search for human values they first lose interest in those natural virtues which serve to keep the structure of the anthill sound; and then when they discover that, even for them as individuals, life has no purpose which their intellects can accept, even they perish of a *taedium vitae* and leave the world to simpler peoples who have still some distance to go before they reach the end of the tether which attaches them to nature. In the drama of history barbarians are always appearing in the rôle of the *deus ex machina,* and the historian is always laying great stress upon "fresh blood" brought in from the provinces or infused by primitive conquerors. And yet he has seldom cared to draw the pessimistic conclusion which alone seems deducible from the facts in his possession.

Nor can it be said that to understand this paradox of humanism helps us in any way to solve it. The analysis which we perform is, indeed, itself an example of one of those exercises of the mind which is perverse because it does not serve as a means toward a natural end, and when we have admitted that the human ideal is one which the human animal cannot even approach without tending to destroy himself as he does so, we have, by that very admission, both diminished our biological fitness and desolated our human feelings. Hence it is that many a man with trained mind, developed sensibilities, and even as much good will toward society as can be expected of a creature who has lost the animal's innate talent for caring more for his race than for himself, stands paralyzed in the midst of a world that has learned so many things which do not help it toward any ultimate solution of its problems but which tend, on the contrary, rather to make him suspect that they are insoluble. These men cannot strive with a missionary zeal for the development and spread of pure science, philosophy, and art because they have come to believe that these things are neither ultimately satisfying nor conducive to a vigorous national life, but neither can they cast their lot with the "plain man," the "sturdy citizen," or the Spartan patriot, because it is the detachment of which these are enemies that gives human life whatever of even doubtful value it seems to the pure humanist to have. To the latter it appears that there is no choice to be made except that between an antlike stability and an eternal recurrence which condemns humanity to a recurrent death at the top, to be followed once more by a fresh growth from the roots.

And, difficult as it seems to him to choose between such unsatisfactory alternatives, he is still further perplexed by an uneasy sense that the decision is one

THREE

The Disillusion with the Laboratory

DURING the second half of the nineteenth century Thomas Henry Huxley delivered a number of lectures, evangelical in character, to popular audiences, and his purpose was a double one. He wished to arouse in his hearers an enthusiasm for the truths of the laboratory equal to his own, but he felt at the same time the necessity of quieting certain fears which had been aroused when Darwinism had exploded in the midst of English society. He was anxious to convince his hearers that the moral fabric of their world was not, as they supposed, put in jeopardy, and he went even so far as to assure them, in effect, that he could give them good human reasons for obeying most of the Ten Commandments even if they should be compelled, as a result of his other teachings, to doubt that these commandments had been handed down to Moses by God Himself.

But there were moments at which he felt himself hard pressed by those of his opponents who doubted the utility, even more than they doubted the truth, of the hypotheses he was expounding. He had received letters from well-meaning old ladies who asked him what *good* it would do to go about assuring people that they had apes rather than angels for cousins-german—even though he himself were sure of the fact —and sometimes he felt the inconvenience of being always compelled to defend his beliefs upon the double ground of their truth *and* usefulness. This inconvenience he did not, however, usually admit in public; but once, just after his son had died and when Charles Kingsley had written him concerning the possibility of a future life, he did, in a private letter, renounce one half of the obligation he usually assumed and, taking his stand upon a dogmatic allegiance to truths of the order which particularly concerned him, he wrote: "Sit down before fact as a little child . . . follow humbly and to whatever abysses Nature leads, or you shall learn nothing."

Now to us of a later day there is something ominous in this sentence. Since the time when first it was defiantly uttered we have listened to the accounts of many explorers who have followed Nature and have returned with tales not wholly reassuring, but we shall miss the contrast between the temper of Huxley's day and our own if we fail to perceive that the words sprang from a heart more confident than the words seem to imply and that, indeed, no utterance of his is more characteristically Victorian. Not only is it marked by a certain rhetorical grandeur which gives it an heroic ring foreign to the best expression in an age like our own, when men have grown a little distrustful of such rotundities, but also, for all the desperation of its rhetoric, it is replete with an unmistakably Victorian optimism. Huxley did not in his heart believe that Nature had any "abysses" very deep or very dark, and he did not really admit the possibility that they might exist. Formally, and for the sake of argument, he declared his willingness to know the worst about man and the universe, but he was serenely confident that that worst was not very bad. He loved what he called Truth, and he believed that all he valued could be established upon it.

This optimism, characteristic of Huxley's age, was the natural accompaniment of a fresh enthusiasm for a new method. Together with those of his contemporaries who had, like him, reflective minds, he per-

ceived that Darwin's discoveries were more than isolated facts, and he saw in them a missing link in the
chain of reasoning which was leading him to the conclusion that all human problems were ultimately solvable. The sciences had already demonstrated their
power to understand and deal with the forces of nature, and now that Darwin had proved that man was
not something essentially different from, but actually
a part of, this same nature, it seemed fair to conclude
that they might hope for an equal success in dealing
with human things. Doubtless he foresaw a part of all
those painstaking studies which have since been made
of the genesis of the arts, religions, and civilizations,
and like those who undertook them he supposed that
they would be as fruitful in both truth and utility as
those of Darwin upon which they were modeled. He
had seen so many problems solved in the laboratory
that he was little disturbed by any doubts as to what
the limits of the method might be, and, while some
were left desolate by theories which seemed to deny
them their trailing clouds of glory, he saw no cause for
anything but hope in an hypothesis which made man
part of that nature which was so rapidly yielding up
its secrets.

In the light of his knowledge and experience Huxley's optimism was not, perhaps, unjustified, but those
of us who look back over the fifty-odd years which
have passed since it expanded in its full flower are
aware of a buoyance which has somehow passed away
and of a sense that the possibility of certain ultimate
solutions has rather receded than approached as the
years went by. All prophecies make sad reading when
their term has elapsed, but in this particular case we
are not quite sure why it should be so, since in so
many respects the optimism of Huxley seems more
than justified. Knowledge *has* marched on—more
rapidly perhaps than he hoped—and this knowledge
has brought with it that increased capacity to control

the accidents of our lives which he predicted. Ingenuity has devised subtler instruments to investigate the
secrets of Nature and to direct her forces than any he
dreamed of; already we know more and can do more
in certain directions than he would have supposed possible for a generation as close as ours is to his own;
and yet, in spite of so much success, we are aware of
a certain disappointment and of a hope less eager than
his, as though our victories were somehow barren and
as though the most essential things were eluding us.
We do not, we cannot, actually doubt even the most
fantastic of the verities which the scientist announces,
since his boasted power to foretell and control upon
the basis of his hypotheses has been too often vindi-
cated to permit a skepticism, and when he tells us that
soon we shall be doing this or that we know from experience that we had best believe him. Yet our belief
is without enthusiasm—even, perhaps, a little perfunc-
tory or impatient—because all his successes seem to
achieve and to promise less than once they did.

Doubtless this disillusion is due in part to a clearer
and clearer penetration of the ancient fallacy which
consists in basing an estimate of our welfare upon the
extent to which our material surroundings have been
elaborated. This fallacy, born at the same moment
with scientific method itself, runs all through the *New
Atlantis* of Bacon, where it leads him to accept without question the assumption that we shall be wise and
happy in proportion to the ingenuity of the machinery
which surrounds us, and it is still the very foundation
stone in the faith of the more naïve of contemporary
materialists who assume that we have, for example,
indubitably bettered ourselves when we have learned,
first to say things over wires, and then to dispense
even with them. A wider and wider experience with
inventions has, however, convinced the more thoughtful that a man is not, as once was said, twice as happy
when moving at the rate of fifty miles an hour as he

would be if he were proceeding at only half that speed, and we no longer believe that the millennium presents merely a problem in engineering. Science has always promised two things not necessarily related—an increase first in our powers, second in our happiness or wisdom, and we have come to realize that it is the first and less important of the two promises which it has kept most abundantly.

Yet this explanation is not in itself complete, and we cannot deny, either, that the better sort of scientist has always realized that the ultimate value of science must depend upon its human value or that his researches into the mind and institutions of man have been less remarkable than those he has conducted into inanimate nature. Huxley himself was fond of pointing out the danger which lay in the error of assuming that a pump was the most important result of our knowledge of the fact that air has weight, or that Galileo was great because he made good clocks possible. He had a Lucretian faith in the power of the light of knowledge to banish the fears which had oppressed the soul of man, and he had, beside, a faith that that same light would so illuminate the moral world as to enable us to see more clearly than we had ever seen before our capacities, our obligations, and our aims. Nature he thought was important chiefly because man was a part of it, and because by knowing nature he would come to know himself. And yet, though the eagerness which the scientist has shown to draw conclusions sociological, ethical, and philosophical from his discoveries is sufficient proof that this aspect of the laboratory has not been forgotten, it is precisely here that our disillusion is keenest.

The more we learn of human nature, the less sure a foundation it seems to be upon which to build; and the more we know of the origins of the arts and faiths which have made the human race seem heroic, the less we see how they can be carried on to any perfection. If

the proud confidence of Huxley has oozed away, it is
in part because the abyss of Nature is darker and
deeper than he supposed, and in part because the light
which illuminates it does not reveal as clearly as he
had anticipated what our bearings are as we wing our
way, like Milton's Satan, through a vast emptiness.
Science, though it fulfills the details of its promises,
does not in any ultimate sense solve our problems.

II

Certainly the spread of scientific method to fields of
inquiry which had not been thought of as subjects
thereto was no less rapid or complete than Huxley
had anticipated. Within a generation people had come
instinctively to assume that the universe was a single
continuity whose phenomena, from the crystallization
of a salt on through the transports of romantic love
or the profoundest experiences of mystical religion,
were all part of the same great system and all natural
in the sense that they were all subject to investigation
by the same methods. Anthropology, defined as the
science of man considered as an animal, was born; and,
though the designation came to be used in a narrow
sense, this definition is sufficient to describe the subject matter of practically every study undertaken during half a century. History, philosophy, and even
theology became chiefly the search for origins and the
study of processes by which things were evolved, so
that even when a man as sympathetic as William
James toward religious experiences undertook to study
them they could only be approached through the
method of documentary comparisons.

First man's body and then his soul were dragged
into the laboratory to be measured, tested, and made
the subject of experiment. His desires, his beliefs, and
his impulses were tracked down, catalogued, and
mapped. The history of morals was written, the physiology of love was described, and the functions of faith

were analyzed. A vast mountain of data, much of it accurate and incontrovertible, upon every activity of the human spirit, was gathered, and always we were promised the great illumination which was to follow its absorption. Knowledge, we had learned, was power. When one had come to understand the laws of physics one was able intelligently to arrange for one's physical well-being, and so when one had learned the laws of the mental world one would be able in the same way to assure one's spiritual state. Once we had come to grasp the principles of art, we should know how to produce it; once we had unraveled the complexities involved in the history of morals, we should be able to devise and practice a really intelligent moral code; and once we thoroughly understood the functions of religion, we should be able to embrace one capable of perfectly fulfilling those functions.

And yet, for some reason not easy at first to comprehend, the analogy has failed to hold, and a laboratory knowledge of what, for want of better terms, we must still speak of as the soul and its activities does not result in any greater mastery of them. Though the "I" in each one of us is the thing of whose reality we seem to have the directest possible evidence, yet in the laboratory it dissolves into an unstable agglomeration of sensations and impulses which we cannot recognize as ourselves, while the "will," which seems to us to inform this nonexistent entity, is revealed as a pure illusion. And if science thus illuminates the problems of the soul by assuring us that it cannot find any of the things we are talking about, its efforts are not much more satisfactory when applied to the study of ethics. A Westermarck, having adopted the genetic methods consecrated by Darwin and having armed himself with the detachment of science, plunges into the study of morals. We eagerly await the exact and positive conclusions which science seems to promise, and he returns with three fat volumes which prove—that morality does not exist. In the laboratory there can be found no trace of the soul except certain rather undignified phenomena which give rise to the illusion that we have one, no sign of the will except that conditioned preponderance of one impulse over the other which leads us to feel as though we were exercising a choice, and no evidence of the existence of any such thing as morality except customs—more or less fixed in certain times or places, but in the large extremely variable—which familiarity leads us to regard as absolute. And yet we act and must act as though these things were realities and the problems which we looked to science to solve were problems predicated upon the real existence of the entities it denies. They are a part of that world—illusory, perhaps—in which our consciousness has its being, even though not part of any which the laboratory can investigate.

The origins, evolutions, and relativities which the latter does reveal are in part disconcerting and in part irrelevant. It has shown itself most competent and most decisive in dealing with those aspects of life which, when contemplated, are the most likely to disturb the equanimity of our souls. It has, that is to say, been most fruitful of result when it has attempted to trace our most exalted feelings back to their basis in some primitive physiological urge; to analyze our art into the elements which serve to excite and satisfy some appetence which seems, when so examined, trivial enough; or to demonstrate how completely our reason—which Shakespeare thought godlike and in which Spinoza thought he had found the realm which he could denominate as "Of Human Freedom"—is in reality also in bondage to our passions and to be adequately described as a mere "rationalization" of them. It has, then, humbled our dignity and clipped the wings of our aspirations, but its disconcerting revelations are more easily borne than the irrelevancies which result from the fact, mentioned above, that the stream of consciousness, and the conditioned preponderance of one impulse over the other with which it replaces the "I" and the "will" of our intimate experience, do not correspond with that experience or help us to understand its problems. To the man in the grip of a romantic passion and uncertain whether "love is all" or merely an infirmity of mind, the modern cure of souls can say no more than that the victim is suffering, perhaps, from a fixation; and the person in search of moral guidance who goes to the scientific studies of morality to get it will be vouchsafed the information that among certain of the South Sea Islanders modesty consists in taking care that the body is tattooed, or that in some other time and place the murder of one's superannuated grandparents was considered a duty. Doubtless the facts in both cases are true, but they are not recognizable in the experience with which the individual is called upon to deal, and they are in that sense irrelevant.

We went to science in search of light, not merely upon the nature of matter, but upon the nature of man as well, and though that which we have received may be light of a sort, it is not adapted to our eyes and is not anything by which we can see. Since thought began we have groped in the dark among shadowy shapes, doubtfully aware of landmarks looming uncertainly here and there—of moral principles, human values, aims, and ideals. We hoped for an illumination in which they would at last stand clearly and unmistakably forth, but instead they appear even less certain and less substantial than before—mere fancies and illusions generated by nerve actions that seem terribly remote from anything we can care about or based upon relativities that accident can shift. We had been assured that many troublesome shadows would flee away, that superstitious fears, irrational repugnances, and all manner of bad dreams would disappear. And so in truth very many have. But we never supposed that most of the things we cherished would prove equally unsubstantial, that all the aims we thought we vaguely perceived, all the values we pursued, and all the principles we clung to were but similar shadows, and that either the light of science is somehow deceptive or the universe, emotionally and spiritually, a vast emptiness.

Hopes are disappointed in strange and unexpected ways. When first we embrace them we fear, if we fear at all, some miscarriage in the details of our plan. We are anxious lest we should not be able to go where we hope to go, acquire what we hope to own, or gain the distinction we hope to win. But it is not thus that we are most frequently or most bitterly disappointed. We accomplish the journeys, assume the possessions, and receive the distinctions, but they are not what we thought them, and in the midst of success it is failure that we taste. It is not the expected thing but the effect that is lost, the advantages of possession or the joys of achievement which fail to materialize, in spite of the fact that it was never at that point that we feared a failure. And so it has been with modern science. It has marched from triumph to triumph, winning each specific victory more completely and more expeditiously than even its most enthusiastic prophet predicted, but those specific victories do not bear the fruits expected. Less follows than once seemed inevitable and we are disillusioned with success.

III

Your scientist, impatient and a little scornful of the speculations, dreams, and fancies which have occupied the man ignorant of the laboratory and its marvels, is inclined to feel sure of his superiority when he insists that it is with *realities* that he deals; but it may be that by that statement he is destroying himself, since the contact of the human mind with reality is so slight that two thousand years of epistemology have not been able to decide exactly what the nexus is, and it is easier to argue that our consciousness exists in utter isolation than to prove that it is actually aware of the external phenomena by which it is surrounded. Nor need we, in order to demonstrate this fact, confine ourselves to the consideration of such intangible things as those which have just been discussed, since the physical world of which we are aware through the senses is almost equally remote from that which the laboratory reveals.

The table before which we sit may be, as the scientist maintains, composed of dancing atoms, but it does not reveal itself to us as anything of the kind, and it is not with dancing atoms but a solid and motionless object that we live. So remote is this "real" table —and most of the other "realities" with which science deals—that it cannot be discussed in terms which have any human value, and though it may receive our purely intellectual credence it cannot be woven into the pattern of life as it is led, in contradistinction to life as we attempt to think about it. Vibrations in the ether are so totally unlike, let us say, the color purple that the gulf between them cannot be bridged, and they are, to all intents and purposes, not one but two separate things of which the second and less "real" must be the most significant for us. And just as the sensation which has led us to attribute an objective reality to a nonexistent thing which we call "purple" is more important for human life than the conception of vibrations of a certain frequency, so too the belief in God, however ill founded, has been more important in the life of man than the germ theory of decay, however true the latter may be.

We may, if we like, speak in consequence, as certain mystics love to do, of the different levels or orders of truth. We may adopt what is essentially a Platonistic trick of thought and insist upon postulating the existence of external realities which corre-

spond to the needs and modes of human feeling and
which, so we may insist, have their being in some part
of the universe unreachable by science. But to do so
is to make an unwarrantable assumption and to be
guilty of the metaphysical fallacy of failing to distinguish between a truth of feeling and that other sort
of truth which is described as a "truth of correspondence," and it is better perhaps, at least for those of
us who have grown up in an age of scientific thought,
to steer clear of such confusions and to rest content
with the admission that, though the universe with
which science deals is the real universe, yet we do not
and cannot have any but fleeting and imperfect con-
tacts with it; that the most important part of our
lives—our sensations, emotions, desires, and aspirations—takes place in a universe of illusions which
science can attenuate or destroy, but which it is powerless to enrich.

But once we have made that admission we must
guard ourselves against the assumption, hastily embraced by those who make the admission too gladly,
that we have thereby liberated ourselves from all
bondage to mere fact and freed the human spirit so
that it may develop in its own way. The human world
is not completely detached and autonomous. Since
mind can function only through body, the one world
is interpenetrated by the other. The two clash from
time to time, and when they do so it is always the
solider which must prevail, so that we dare not attempt to deny its existence. The world which our
minds have created to meet our desires and our needs
exists precariously and on sufferance; it is shadowy
and insubstantial for the very reason that there is
nothing outside itself to correspond with it, and hence
it must always be fragile and imperfect.

Science, to be sure, has sometimes imagined a wholly
scientific man of the future, and the more thorough-

going sort of scientist has sometimes predicted that the time would come when the world of the human mind would be precisely the world of the laboratory and nothing more. Conceiving a daily life far more thoroughly mechanized than that of today—of a society that sped through the air at incredible speed, that took its nourishment in the form of concentrated pellets, and generated its children from selected seeds in an annealed glass womb—he has imagined a man possessed of a soul fit for such surroundings. To him the needs and emotions referred to in this essay as distinctly human are merely troublesome anachronisms destined to pass away when we have accustomed ourselves more completely to things as they are, and it is our business to get rid of them as rapidly as possible in order to hasten the coming of the happy being to whom the roar of wheels will be the sweetest melody and a laboratory the only tabernacle for which he feels any need.

But it must be remembered that before such a creature could come into being changes more fundamental than are sometimes imagined would have to take place, since, even if we confine our attention to his physical surroundings only, he would have to be one who lived no longer, as all of us do, in the world of appearances, but one for whom vibrations were more real than colors because the spectroscope and the interferometer were more natural than the eye. For him the table in its most intimate aspect would have to be a swarm of dancing atoms, and not only all the art but all the thought and feeling of past humanity alien nonsense. We could understand him no more than we now understand the ant on the one hand or the dynamo on the other, and he would feel no kinship with us. And hence, though we may admit the possibility that the future belongs to him, we cannot feel any delight in it or make its possessor any concern of ours. It is to our humanity that we cling, because it is the thing which we recognize as ourselves, and if it is lost, then all that counts for us is lost with it.

What we have come to realize, then, is that the scientific optimism of which Huxley may be taken as a typical exponent was merely a new variety of faith, resting upon certain premises which are no more unassailable than those which have supported other vanished religions of the past. It had as its central dogma the assumption that truths (of correspondence) were necessarily useful, and that the human spirit flowered best in the midst of realities clearly perceived. After the manner of all religions, it instinctively refrained from any criticism of this essential dogma, and it was left to us in an age troubled by a new agnosticism to perceive how far this first article of the scientific creed is from being self-evidently true. Experience has taught us that the method of the laboratory has its limitation and that the accumulation of scientific data is not, in the case of all subjects, useful. We have learned how certain truths—intimate revelations concerning the origin and mechanism of our deepest impulses—can stagger our souls, and how a clear perception of our lonely isolation in the midst of a universe which knows nothing of us and our aspirations paralyzes our will. We are aware, too, of the fact that art and ethics have not flowered anew in the light, that we have not won a newer and more joyous acceptance of the universe, and we have come to realize that the more we learn of the laws of that universe— in which we constitute a strange incongruity—the less we shall feel at home in it.

Each new revelation fascinates us. We would not, even if we dared, remain ignorant of anything which we can learn, but with each new revelation we perceive so much the more clearly that half—perhaps the most important half—of all we are and desire to be can find no comfort or support in such knowledge, that it is useless to seek for correspondences between our inner world and the outer one when we know that no such correspondences exist. Many of the things which we value most have a relation to external nature no more intimate than the relation of purple to vibrations of the ether, and the existence of such a relation can never be to us more than an academic fact. We are disillusioned with the laboratory, not because we have lost faith in the truth of its findings but because we have lost faith in the power of those findings to help us as generally as we had once hoped they might help.

IV

And what, then, of the Age of Science? It began, perhaps, with the Renaissance, or perhaps with the beginning of the seventeenth century, which saw the first of its most magnificent triumphs, and it may not yet have reached its apogee. Is it destined to give way to some other age, named from some new predominant interest? Will it be looked back upon as an epoch whose limits, like the limits of others, can be recognized? Or is it, as some seem to think, a period which began when, for the first time, the true method of inquiry was discovered, and which is hence certain to endure as long as the continuity of life is maintained? Is it something with a beginning, but no other end than the end of the story of mankind?

Not even a speculative answer can be given to that question unless we define more closely what we mean when we ask it, and certainly it is not likely that the time will ever come when the wheels of the machine will cease to turn or the door of the laboratory be closed. Fanatics, the antithesis of those who gladly envisage a more and more vertiginously mechanized world, have been known to express a wish that just that would happen. So violently have they hated the soul of the modern man that they have wished to erase from the record of history every thought and deed since the Renaissance, and have longed for the return of a new Middle Age hardly different from that which closed when new hopes were born.

But one need not have all of Huxley's faith to see the absurdity of such a program. One can hardly embrace it without being willing at the same time to destroy a large part of the population of the earth, because only the devices of science make it possible for them to be supported; and, even if one accepted that condition, one can hardly wish for the return of those good old days when there was nothing but prayer to oppose to the ravishes of a plague or when a wounded limb rotted slowly but inevitably away. There is something to be grateful for also in the fact, for which the realism of science is largely responsible, that we are no longer likely to be burned at the stake because we hold too tenaciously an unpopular opinion concerning the nature of the Trinity which we feel it would involve damnation to relinquish, and there are other benefits bestowed by science which we are not anxious to surrender. If we speak, then, of the possibility that the Age of Science may pass, we do not mean that science would thereupon cease to perform its functions. We are thinking rather of a time when those boundless hopes which Huxley cherished, and to which many still cling, shall have been definitely renounced, when science shall no longer be looked to as the universal nostrum, and when it shall no longer give its name to an epoch because it will no longer be the dominant interest of all the best minds.

Even this is not easy for us, born as we were in the midst of an age of faith, to imagine. We have grown accustomed both to the triumphs of science and to the gradual extension of its activities, until they have come to seem to us something inevitable. We can hardly conceive how they should cease to occur or by what process the tendencies they express should pass away; and yet, if we follow the method which science has taught us, if we will make a study of comparative intellectual religions, we may see how that which happened once may come about again.

There was once, as every one knows, a time when deduction, or the method of metaphysics, had followers as devoted, as numerous, and as confident as ever were won by the rival system of inductive logic upon which science is based. The universities of the Middle Ages which sprang up over Europe and were filled with eager scholars were an expression of the extravagant hopes which the world then fastened upon the methods of the schoolmen just as surely as the laboratories now dotting the face of the earth are an expression of the hopes which science has inspired. In that day students flocked to the centers from obscure corners just as they do now, and they were drawn for the same reason. Keen minds were attacking the most important problems which face mankind with a new weapon, and the syllogism was marching from triumph to triumph. Every problem seemed to yield to the strength of that mighty engine, a thrill not unlike that which we feel at the successful result of a new experiment went through the soul of the listening world of scholars when a new demonstration was achieved, and it seemed as though everything were ultimately knowable. Vast volumes, filled with certitudes and no less imposing in bulk than those our own age has produced, were written; and at last came one who summarized in one great work a systematic series of answers to all the questions a wise man would care to ask.

Little remains as a result of all this activity. Most of the writings it produced are couched in a jargon which only the specialized student can understand, and the veriest amateur of science will tell you, with a quiet confidence based upon a complete ignorance of the subject, that the schoolmen wasted their time.

And how came it, then, that that which once seemed the greatest of human triumphs has sunk so low in the estimation of the world that few take even the trouble to find out what it was? Somehow the confidence which had been reposed in it oozed away and there was a growing disillusion with the metaphysician not unlike that disillusion which is the subject of the present essay. Within its own world metaphysics was perfect, but it came to seem, like so much of modern science, less relevant to the life people led than at first it appeared to be. Men's realest needs and desires seemed to elude it, and the progress which it made was the progress of a squirrel in its cage. Its irrefutable demonstrations made very little difference in the success of the lives of those who mastered them, and enthusiasm waned, not so much because of any failure upon which it was possible to put one's finger as because metaphysics did not seem to be helping people very rapidly along the road which they wished to travel.

And if we were compelled to sum up our criticism of modern science in a single phrase we could hardly find one better than this last—that it does not seem, so surely as once it did, to be helping us very rapidly along the road we wish to travel. We cannot make physical speed an end to be pursued very long after we have discovered that it does not get us anywhere, and neither can we long devote ourselves whole-heartedly to science except in those departments—like medicine, for example—that accomplish not merely results, but results which have an ultimate value.

This does not mean, as some are already suggesting, that we have reason to return with a new enthusiasm to metaphysics. The fact that science has not succeeded in many of her efforts does not make the failure of the schoolmen any less evident; does not prove, for example, that he who finds Westermarck unsatisfactory will find what he is looking for in the pages of Saint Thomas. But it does mean, on the other hand, that the new instrument has begun, like the old, to reveal its limitations, and that our aim has once more eluded us. Huxley and the schoolman were essentially alike in that the ultimate aim of each was the establishment of a science of man founded upon an accurate and positive knowledge of his nature; and they were alike also in the fact that the failure of each served to demonstrate that human nature is too phantasmagorical, too insubstantial, too "unreal" to submit to such treatment, that it must continue to exist precariously and, as it were, upon sufferance in a universe not made for it. It may be that in time the most honored volumes which the scientific study of human nature has produced will become as nearly unread as the *Summa Theologiae* itself, even though, in some still more distant future, they are rediscovered and revived in one of those oscillations of ever disappointed hope such as that which, at the present moment, is leading not a few back to Saint Thomas.

FOUR

Love—or the Life and
Death of a Value

In one of those popular phrases too generally current to be attributed to any particular person, and hence seeming to have been uttered by a whole and united folk, our Victorian ancestors were accustomed to say that "love is best." Perhaps no other cultural group had ever set itself more resolutely to discipline this most unruly of passions by laying down the conditions under which one might permissibly indulge in it, and perhaps no other had expressed a more inflexible disapproval of any violation of the taboos with which it was surrounded; but, for all the strictness of its definition, it gave to "virtuous love" the highest place in its hierarchy of values.

The age was, though we sometimes forget the fact, an age of many skepticisms, during which many things were called in question but it never doubted the worth of that which we are accustomed to call, in a phrase whose downrightness would have shocked it profoundly, "sublimated sex." It looked with loathing and fear at any of the cruder manifestations of the sexual instincts, but when those instincts had been adorned with poetry, and submitted to the discipline of society, it regarded them as the source not only of the most admirable virtues but of the most intrinsically valuable of human experiences as well. In theory, at least, a successful love crowned all other successes and obliterated all other failures. It made all men equal because all men were capable of it, and it stood between man and any ultimate pessimism because, so long as love was possible, life could not be either meaningless or not worth the living. Nor was this evaluation questioned by the leaders in any school of thought, for upon this point even Gladstone and Huxley would have agreed. Whether man were son of God or great-grandson of the ape, it was in love that he fulfilled himself. If he were the former, then love brought him nearer than anything else to the divine state from which he had fallen; if he were the latter, then at least love carried him to the highest level of which he was capable.

Now faiths such as this lie deeper than religious or political creeds. The Christian knows that he is a Christian and that other people are not; the democrat is aware of theories of government other than his; but such tacit evaluations as that set upon love are accepted as matters of fact, almost as something established by the scheme of nature. These Victorians knew that they were, in the literal sense of the word, puritans here as elsewhere. They knew, that is to say, that they had insisted upon a soberness in love as well as in religion, and that they looked upon the antisocial tendencies of extravagant passion in the same way that they looked upon the antisocial tendencies of extravagant religion; but that it was in love that the meaning of life must inevitably be sought they never stopped to doubt. They did not much consider the fact that the ability to live for love in any form was a relatively recent accomplishment on the part of the human race; that the tacit assumption which lay behind all their literature and all their thinking was not, after all, part of the unchangeable nature of man but merely an assumption, seemingly inevitable because it had been handed on and accepted by one generation after another, which had changed the rules of the game but never doubted that it was worth the playing. And it was in part because love seemed to them so inevitably valuable that they were able to hold so firmly to their belief in its supreme importance.

We, however, have specialized in origins, and it requires no more than a glance at the past to show that the high values set upon love are not inevitable. Certainly the savage—the American Indian, for example—knows comparatively little of what we call romance. When he sings his songs or addresses his gods, when, that is to say, his consciousness reaches the intensest level of which he is capable, it is upon thoughts of agriculture and of war that he most often dwells. These are the activities which seem to him to be most worthy to be realized or adorned in contemplation, because they are the ones which seem to bring him closest to the meaning of life; and when he thinks of wooing he does so chiefly not because he regards love as the most significant of human emotions but because his wife will bear him sons to help guide the destiny of the tribe or to slay its enemies. Like all human beings, the savage considers certain experiences as ends in themselves, but he still regards the act of sexual union as a relatively simple process, important chiefly because of its biological function; it is only somewhere between savagery and civilization that love is born.

At first it holds, no doubt, a relatively low place in the hierarchy of values. The stories which deal with it are at first fewer than those which deal with the struggle against the elements and warfare with neighboring tribes; the lover is still far less than the warrior the type of the hero; and soft emotions are still a matter for surprise, almost for shame. But once these emotions have been accepted into song and story, they reveal an amazing capacity to elaborate and complicate themselves. They come to be regarded with respect and awe; a mythology quite as elaborate as that concerning the combats of warriors grows up around them; and tacitly it is assumed that a great love is a subject hardly less worthy, hardly less near the divine, than a great heroism.

Perhaps the sterner members of the society set themselves up against it and shake their heads when amorous songs or poems win more applause than warlike ones, but at least the romantic view of life has come to set itself against what, for want of a better name, we must call the heroic one, and a value is born.

Love is, then, not a fact in nature of which we become aware, but rather a creation of the human imagination; and this is true not only when we think of the word as implying some complicated system of attitudes like that of the Victorians, but even when we think of it as referring to no more than a mere physical act to which considerable importance is attached. The very singling out of this particular desire as one more significant than others must precede any attribution of transcendental values to it, and even this singling out took place recently enough for us to be aware of it. If mere lust cannot play any very large part in human life until the imagination has created it, how much more conspicuously is it true that we must regard as purely a creation of the human mind so complex a system of emotional attitudes—interwoven with all sorts of aesthetic sociological and mystical conceptions—as that which was implied by the Victorian in the word "love." Behind the simple phrase "love is best" lies a history—half of social organization, half of human imagination—which volumes could not adequately trace.

Yet, artificial as is this system of values, and fundamentally illogical as are the associations which lead us to center the chief human experiences around love, they tend strongly to perpetuate themselves, both because the young of a nation become habituated to an acceptance of them long before any critical sense is developed and because, so far as they are the result of any biologically transmutable evolution, the development of the race is recapitulated in that of the individual. As a child, the normal individual is, like the savage on all but special occasions, either almost unaware of sex or inclined to regard it as something between the ludicrous, the forbidden, and the obscene. He is ashamed of any unexpected emotion which he feels in the presence of his complement, and he is inclined to jeer at those slightly older than himself who show any tendency to abandon the—to him—rational preoccupations of childhood. But then, as he reaches adolescence, a change no less surprising to himself than to others takes place. Much that, as a child, he had heard without understanding becomes suddenly meaningful to him, and he realizes that he is capable of participating in experiences which have hitherto been known to him only by the words applied to them. All his daydreams now center around exploits which a little before would have seemed to him silly, and if he happens to have been born into one of those highly developed societies, like our own, where love is often regarded as the supreme human privilege, he will invest thoughts of that which had been, a short time before, both ridiculous and obscene with a religious awe.

Not only will his thoughts be constantly busy with it, but he will tend to center around it even those of his aspirations which do not seem to be actually related. He will plan to become virtuous, brave, and successful in order to please some member of the opposite sex; he will achieve wealth, power, or fame in order to lay them at her feet. Even those things which earlier—and perhaps also later—seem to him quite worth having for themselves must now borrow their value from her. The ramifications of a simple biological act have come to fill the universe, and it, with all that it involves, has come to be not merely one of the things which make life worth while, but *the* thing which at all justifies or makes it meaning-ful. For him, as for his race, love has, in a word, be-come a value—perhaps the supreme one—something indubitably worth while in itself and something capa-ble by its own magic of making other things valuable either as means or as adornments.

Such a youth has come into an inheritance of illu-sions as important and perhaps as valuable as any-thing else which his ancestors have transmitted to him. He accepts it as part of nature, but it is, as surely as the government under which he lives or the house which shelters him, a human creation, and one which is more fundamental than any other because it is not something which enables him to live but something which endows living with a meaning and a purpose. It is an illusion to which centuries of existence have been necessary before it could assume the form and the apparent solidity with which to him it seems endowed, a value which was gradually created while other values faded away.

To the savage who knew nothing of romantic love the world was not so barren without it as it would seem under similar circumstances to the average Latin or Teuton of our day. The experiences of the hunt, still lingeringly delightful to many, were to him pas-sionately absorbing and intrinsically as worth while as love-making later came to be. In the celebration of the spring festival he had as ecstatic a sense of a mysti-cal initiation into the meaning of the universe as the modern young romantic for the first time in the arms of his mistress. But the possibility of these experiences has passed away.

While love was gradually being created, other values vanished; for such, for all their apparent inevitability to those who feel them, is their way; and to know this is to know that even the complex of illusions called "love" is one which might also, under certain circum-stances, pass away. Certain peoples, it is obvious, have never had it. Consider, for example, the mental and social organization not only of the savage but of, let us say, the Chinese, whose entire spiritual life is fundamentally incomprehensible to us largely because of the fact that, having always regarded sexual passion as a relatively trivial thing, they have set the highest value upon filial rather than upon marital love, and about this latter have centered not only their social structure but the most important of their moral and emotional groupings as well, so that, for example, they would not be, like us, inclined to think of love as the chief source of virtue or the chief reward of fortitude.

Nor do we need, in order to get some faint idea how love might come to be less for us than it was for our ancestors, go so far afield as savagery or China, since we may observe in the lives of our own not too remote forefathers how certain self-justifying and intrinsically worth-while activities came to lose their magic. From certain pursuits—war, for example—they got satisfactions which, at least so far as the more advanced part of mankind is concerned, we find it difficult to understand. Of it, of chivalric honor, of national glory, of noble birth, and of various other things, they spoke in a way which indicates that these things had for them an emotional content which is rapidly becoming as nearly extinct as that which is embodied for the savage in the spring festival and which it is almost as hard for us to understand as it would be for a Chinese sage to understand what we mean when we speak of a "world well lost for love."

Values of this kind seem so inevitably natural to those who accept them, and pass so insensibly away, that their rise and fall are only imperfectly recorded, but the changes which take place in their status are, perhaps, the most momentous events in the life of the human race. They have a far more profound effect upon man than any mere changes of government, for they are, in effect, changes of God, and they involve a change both in his whole conception of the meaning of the universe and in the thing for which he lives. Every time a value is born, existence takes on a new meaning; every time one dies, some part of that meaning passes away.

II

Most of the faiths which we received from the Victorians had already by then been shaken. Certainly the church which they left us was already weakened and despoiled, and the majority of their dogmas had become gradually so much attenuated that it needed only the resolution "Pooh!" uttered by the new generation to make them vanish away. Yet their religion of love, or at least the value which they attached to that passion, reached us almost intact. With no subject has the contemporary mind been more persistently busy, but it did not, in the beginning, think of questioning the fundamental premise.

If one reads the novels of H. G. Wells—which will stand as perhaps the best expression of the minds of the "liberal" mass—one will see that for all their social iconoclasm they imply a tacit acceptance of the assumption that "love is best" quite as complete as that of any Victorian novel; and if one reads the six volumes of Havelock Ellis's *Studies in the Psychology of Sex*—which will stand perhaps as the completest and most characteristic of those works which made a rationalist attitude toward sex an important feature of the spirit of the age—one will see that to Ellis, too, love has its element of transcendental value. Neither the scientist nor the romancer dreamed of questioning the fact that love was the most significant of human experiences and that in it men might find the ultimate justification of life. If both were frequently concerned with an attack upon what were beginning to be called, even in popular language, the "taboos" which

surround the theory and the practice of love, both were
so concerned because they thought of love as too obviously the supreme privilege of man to be burdened
with irrational proscriptions; and their ultimate purpose was, in a word, not to cheapen or tarnish, but
merely to free it.

The Victorians, for all their romantic system of
values, had accepted the frustrations and the sacrifices
entailed by their social code with a complacency which
seemed to the new generation hardly less than heart-
less. They had seemed to take even a sort of perverse
satisfaction in contemplating the bowed head with
which people were supposed to acknowledge the in-
violability of the rules and which Matthew Arnold
had celebrated in two of his most characteristic stan-
zas:

> Each in his own strict line we move,
> And some find death ere they find love;
> So far apart their lives are thrown
> From the twin soul that halves their own.

> And sometimes, by still harder fate,
> The lovers meet, but meet too late
> —Thy heart is mine; *True, true. Ah, true.*
> —Then, love, thy hand; *Ah, no! Adieu!*

They had, moreover, visited their punishments
mercilessly, and they had even—witness George Eliot
in *Adam Bede*—persuaded themselves that the punishments visited by society upon those who violated its
taboos were the result of a law of nature, and the new
generation was merely anxious to avoid the commoner
tragedies of love which it regarded as avoidable. It
looked forward to an individual who, free from a cor-
roding sense of sin, should live in a society which
placed no unnecessary restrictions upon emotional fulfillment, and, far from anticipating any cynical deval-
uation of love itself, it hoped only for an age in which

men should love more freely, more fully, and more perfectly.

Yet it requires no more than a casual acquaintance with either contemporary life or its reflection in contemporary literature to enable one to perceive that this life hardly corresponds to the anticipation.

Freedom has come, but with it a certain lessened sense of the importance of the passions that are thus freely indulged; and if love has come to be less often a sin it has come also to be less often a supreme privilege. If one turns to the smarter of those novelists who describe the doings of the more advanced set of those who are experimenting with life—to, for example, Aldous Huxley or Ernest Hemingway—one will discover in their tragic farces the picture of a society which is at bottom in despair because, though it is more completely absorbed in the pursuit of love than in anything else, it has lost the sense of any ultimate importance inherent in the experience which preoccupies it; and if one turns to the graver of the intellectual writers—to, for example, D. H. Lawrence, T. S. Eliot, or James Joyce—one will find both explicitly and implicitly a similar sense that the transcendental value of love has become somehow attenuated, and that, to take a perfectly concrete example a conclusion which does no more than bring a man and woman into complete possession of one another is a mere bathos which does nothing except legitimately provoke the comment, "Well, what of it?" One can hardly imagine them concerned with what used to be called, in a phrase which they have helped to make faintly ridiculous, "the right to love." Individual freedom they have inherited and assumed as a right, but they are concerned with something which their more restricted forefathers assumed—with, that is to say, the value of love itself. No inhibitions either within or without restrain them, but they are asking themselves, "What is it worth?" and they are certainly no longer feeling that it is obviously and in itself something which makes life worth the living.

To Huxley and Hemingway—I take them as the most conspicuous exemplars of a whole school—love is at times only a sort of obscene joke. The former in particular has delighted to mock sentiment with physiology, to place the emotions of the lover in comic juxtaposition with quaint biological lore, and to picture a romantic pair "quietly sweating palm to palm." But the joke is one which turns quickly bitter upon the tongue, for a great and gratifying illusion has passed away, leaving the need for it still there. His characters still feel the physiological urge and, since they have no sense of sin in connection with it, they yield easily and continually to that urge; but they have also the human need to respect their chief preoccupation, and it is the capacity to do this that they have lost. Absorbed in the pursuit of sexual satisfaction, they never find love and they are scarcely aware that they are seeking it, but they are far from content with themselves. In a generally devaluated world they are eagerly endeavoring to get what they can in the pursuit of satisfactions which are sufficiently instinctive to retain inevitably a modicum of animal pleasure, but they cannot transmute that simple animal pleasure into anything else. They themselves not infrequently share the contempt with which their creator regards them, and nothing could be less seductive, because nothing could be less glamorous, than the description of the debaucheries born of nothing except a sense of the emptiness of life.

Now it is gratifyingly appropriate that this Huxley should be the grandson of the great Victorian exponent of life rationally conducted in the light of natural knowledge, since the predicament which he recognizes is a direct result of the application of the principles advocated by the grandfather. It is true, of course, that Thomas Henry Huxley felt too strongly the influence of Victorian taboos ever to indulge in any extended naturalistic consideration of the problems of sex, but the Ellises and the Wellses, whom we have taken as the type of those who have concerned themselves with such an effort, did little more than apply the principles which he laid down. They used analysis in an effort to clarify an illusion, and the result, which now seems as though it might have been foretold, was to destroy that illusion.

They were, to be sure, successful in the immediate objects which they proposed to themselves; they did, that is to say, succeed in freeing love, both by relaxing somewhat the ferocity with which society had punished conduct which deviated from even the mere letter of its code and by lifting from mankind the burden of that sense of guilt which had oppressed so many and not infrequently poisoned what would have been otherwise a mighty and perfect experience. But when the consequences of love were made less momentous, then love itself became less momentous too, and we have discovered that the now-lifted veil of mystery was that which made it potentially important as well as potentially terrible. Sex, we learned, was not so awesome as once we had thought; God does not care so much about it as we had formerly been led to suppose; but neither, as a result, do we. Love is becoming gradually so accessible, so unmysterious, and so free that its value is trivial.

That which the Victorians regarded as possessed of a supreme and mystical value was, as we have already pointed out, a group of related ideas and emotional attitudes whose elements had, during a long period of time, been associated by means of connections not always logical. Analysis can dissociate them and has indeed done so, but in so doing it destroys the importance which only as a group they possessed. We know that the social consequences which once followed a surrender to love need no longer do so, and hence the nexus between the sexual act and those elements of the love complex which are predominantly social has disappeared. More important yet, we know, or rather we feel, that this act is a simple biological one which sends no reverberations through a spiritual universe, and so it no longer has any transcendental implications. With vertiginous rapidity it is being reduced to that which it was in savage or prehuman society, and threatens to become again no more than a simple physiological act with no more than a simple physiological act's importance or value.

For many generations the adolescence of the individual has repeated the miracle achieved in the first place by the human race as a whole; it has, that is to say, associated the new impulses suddenly discovered in itself with various duties to society and with all the other aspirations of which it is capable; but this miracle is one which is becoming constantly more difficult of performance. Certain individuals have always and for different reasons failed to achieve it, and they have been compelled in consequence to lead jangled lives; but more and more people find themselves victims of a disharmony which results from the fact that they cannot escape a continual preoccupation with a passion which seems to their intellect trivial, and it would not be wholly fanciful to say that this sense of disharmony, of the unworthiness of their aims, is the modern equivalent of the conviction of sin.

It is not to be supposed, I take it, that any mood so disrupted as this is destined to endure. It represents an unstable equilibrium of forces in which one or the other is bound sooner or later to yield; for if the passion of love is to be devaluated, then it must be made to play in human life a part as small as our slight estimate of its importance makes appropriate. Such was the position to which the early Church Fathers attempted to reduce it, and they were unsuccessful because the conflict which they felt between their instincts and their intellectual convictions was resolved in the religion of love; but the modern consciousness is surely destined either to evolve some equally mighty fiction or, while surrendering the erotic instinct as a source of important values, to dispose of it in some fashion involving a minimum of inconvenience and distraction. Nor is the fact that the ferocious and deliberate nastiness of some current writers suggests that of the Fathers, that, for example, Huxley has even in the midst of one of his novels quoted in the Latin from which he hardly dared translate it one of the most brutally scornful of their comments upon the flesh, merely an accident. There is a certain similarity between the early saint and the contemporary sophisticate which is due to the fact that, however different their experiences may be, each rejects love for the same reason—each, that is to say, has refused to surround it with mystical implications and each, looking at it as a mere biological fact, has found it ridiculous and disgusting. Certainly the nastiness of, let us say, James Joyce's *Ulysses* is the nastiness of an ascetic reviling the flesh in order that he may be free of it.

Now, if we set aside the ascetic ideal which in the past, at least, has generally proved itself radically impracticable, and if we set aside also the romantic ideal which the rationalizing tendencies of the human mind seem certain to destroy, there is only one way in which the artist—by which term is here meant whoever is distinctly human enough to have a plan for his life which he sets up in opposition to the simple plan of Nature—may deal with sex, and that way is the one in which it is accepted as something ineluctable, perhaps, but nevertheless uncomplex and trivial. The man who follows it may feel no need to battle against the flesh; he may have no desire to waste his energies in a futile struggle against the inclinations of the natural man, and he may preach no stern denials; but he makes of love a game, a joke, a ribaldry even, in order that, since it no longer seems really significant, it may be reduced to a mere incident.

And if, leaving the Huxleys and the Hemingways, who are concerned with characters still in the midst of confusion, we turn to certain other novelists, poets, and critics, we shall find them at least adumbrating such a solution, as may be illustrated by the words put into the mouth of a by no means ascetic painter in one of the most powerful of contemporary novels. "The tendency of my work," he remarks, "is, as you may have noticed, that of an invariable severity. Apart from its being good or bad, its character is ascetic rather than sensuous, and divorced from immediate life. There is no slop of sex in *that*."

Such a character is merely the novelist's projection of a type which logically results from the effort to think one's way through the confusions just outlined. This painter—Tarr is his name—represents the direction in which we are moving, and he explains the growing popularity of abstract design in the plastic arts and of pure intellectualism in literature, since both represent a reaction from that diffusion of sublimated sex through all the arts which is one of the chief characteristics of romanticism. But however logical and inevitable such a tendency may be, and however preferable it is to an absorption in things which can no longer be respected, it must be remembered that it is, nevertheless, based upon a complete surrender of something which we have been accustomed to regard as one of the chief values in human life, and that it leaves a mighty blank in existence.

Whatever else love may still be—game, puerility, or wry joke played by the senses and the imagination upon the intellect—it no longer is the ultimate self-justifying value which once it was. We may still on occasion surrender to it, but surrender is no longer a paradoxical victory and the world is no longer well lost for love.

Many other things we have come to doubt—patriotism, self-sacrifice, respectability, honor—but in the general wreck the wreck of love is conspicuous and typical. Rationalism having destroyed the taboos which surrounded it, and physiology having rudely investigated its phenomena upon the same level as other biological processes, it has been stripped of the mystical penumbra in whose shadow its transcendental value seemed real, though hid; and somehow, in the course of the very process of winning the right to love, love itself has been deprived of its value.

Such, in outline, is the process by which is accomplished what has here been called the death of a value. Many of us, not yet old, were born at a time when the religion of love was all but unquestioned, when it seemed to stand more firmly than even the religion of the church, whose foundations science was already known slowly to have undermined. But if we have followed the course of modern thought we have seen it rapidly disintegrate. We have seen how works, of which Havelock Ellis's *magnum opus* is a type, claimed love as a legitimate subject for rationalistic consideration, and how, though Ellis himself believed that the superstructure of poetry would remain after its foundations had been subject to rational examination, just as Thomas Huxley believed that the superstructure of Christian morality would stand after the supernatural props had been removed from under it, the mystical values lingered as ghosts for only one generation after rationalism had attacked the mythology upon which they rested.

We have seen the rise of an atheism quite as significant in the history of the human soul as that which has regard to religion in the more conventional sense, and one whose result may be summed up by a consideration of the fact that, though the phrase "love is best" meant to our grandfathers more things than a volume could describe, it is to us so completely denuded that we can only repeat it as we repeat one of those formulae of theology which, though once rich with meaning, are to us only words, words, words.

III

Others who have described, though perhaps in somewhat different terms, the disintegration of the love complex have been concerned chiefly with its effect upon human society. They have stressed their fear that, for example, the progressive tendency to dissociate love from family life would involve the most thoroughgoing reconstruction of our social organization, even if it did not destroy the possibility of any stable society, and in general they have thought of modified sexual customs in terms of their effect upon the race. We, however, are here concerned with the individual and with the consequences which the process we have been describing may have for the intimate emotional life of the separate soul—with, in a word, the changes involved by the death of love in the character of what we may call the experience of living.

We will, if we must, give up the illusion of love. The time may come when it will mean to us even less than it now means to the philosophical Chinese and no more than it did to the savage; when, to state the case somewhat differently, romance will be, either as a motive in art or an aim in living, as fundamentally incomprehensible to us as it is to the Oriental sage, and when it will be so, not because we have not yet developed the complex system of associations upon which it depends, but because the analytical tendencies of our intelligence forbid our imagination to create the values once deemed so precious.

We may realize now that the effort to develop the possibilities of love as an adornment of life by understanding it more completely wrecks itself upon the fact that to understand any of the illusions upon which the values of life depend inevitably destroys them; but we realize the fact too late, and even if we should convince ourselves that we have paid too high a price for our rationality, that we should willingly reassume all the taboos of the Victorian if we could feel again his buoyant sense that the meaning of life had been revealed to him through love, we could no more recapture his illusions by means of an intellectual conviction than we could return to the passionate faith of the Middle Ages merely because, having read Ruskin, we should like to build a cathedral.

Nor is human life so rich in values as to justify us in surrendering any one of them complacently. At bottom, life is worth living only because certain of our conscious activities allowed themselves to be regarded as though they were possessed of some importance or significance in themselves, and even the number of such conscious activities is too strictly limited to permit us to accept without foreboding the reduction of so important a one as that of sexual union to the status of a mere triviality. Many of the life processes—and by no means the least important—are carried on without the accompaniment of any awareness whatsoever. The beating of the heart and the slow churning of the stomach, to say nothing of the infinitely complicated activities with which the glands are busy, are as little a part of that consciousness which we know of as ourselves as is the shifting of the earth upon its axis or the explosive disintegration of an atom of radium. In one sense man cannot either "know himself" or "live completely," for the simple reason that only a fragment of his total organism is connected with that part of the brain wherein resides all that he is accustomed to call his ego or self. The body keeps itself alive by processes which we neither will nor recognize, and death may be preparing itself for months before a warning finally bursts its way into that relatively small mass of cells to which our awareness and hence our emotions confine themselves. When the life of any individual rises above the dim level of the mere toiler whose existence is scarcely more than a round of duties, and reaches that distinctly human level upon which contemplation in some form or other furnishes the motive for living, it does so because he has attributed a meaningfulness to some aspect of consciousness, but the possibilities for such attribution are limited.

Eating, because it is a conscious and not an unconscious process, because the taste buds of the tongue happen to be connected by nerves with the cerebrum and not the cerebellum, can be made into one of the ceremonies by which life is elaborated and can pass as a symbol into poetry and philosophy. So, for the same reason, can the act of sexual union; but both digestion and gestation, because they are controlled without the intervention of consciousness, are destined to remain merely unadorned processes of nature. Man has wanted to live in order to love or even in order to eat, but hardly in order either to gestate or to digest. Yet it is merely an accident of our nervous organization that this is so.

Thus it is that of the infinitely complicated processes of life, in the biological sense, only a few are subject to that elaboration and poetization which make them even potentially a part of significant human experience. Just as the ears can hear only a certain limited class of the innumerable kinds of waves which roll incessantly through the air, and the eyes can see only a certain few of those vibrations in the ether which, after ranging from red to violet, pass on into invisibility, so, too, only a few of the processes of life furnish materials available to the mind. From a limited number of colors we must paint our pictures, from a limited number of sounds we compose our symphonies, and from a limited number of conscious processes construct our "good life." But we are no more aware through our minds of the totality of what living involves than we are through our sense of the entire natural world. To ultra-violet light we are as blind as a man without eyes, and, similarly, most of our biological existence is as meaningless to us as the life of an insect is to it. Whatever does not happen within a few square inches upon the surface of our forebrain does not, so far as we are concerned, happen at all. It cannot be made the source of any human value, because it is a part of us which lives as the plant lives, without any knowledge of itself.

Nature, then, has imposed a certain rigid selection upon us. Grudgingly, perhaps, she has permitted us to be aware of certain of her activities, and has bid us do what we may by way of contemplating or elaborating them until they seem to become not, as to her all things are, merely the means by which life is kept going but ends to be enjoyed or valued in themselves. Within the limits which she has set we have, moreover, made certain choices of our own. Certain of the available conscious processes have seemed to us more suitable than others for this contemplation or elaboration, and we have devoted ourselves to them, leaving the others merely upon the fringe of awareness. Thus we made mere animal combativeness into chivalry, surrounded lair-making with all the associations which belong to the idea of home, and created a sense of the presence of God out of the fears for our security; but the greatest and most elaborate of our creations was love, and the process by which it is stripped of its meaning is a process by which man is dehumanized and life is made to sink back to a level nearer that of the animal, for whom life is a phenomenon in which there is no meaning except the biological urge.

At the very least it means that a color has faded from our palette, a whole range of effects dropped out of our symphony. Intellectually we may find romantic people and romantic literature only ridiculous, intellectually we may convince ourselves that we regret the passing of love no more than the passing of the spring festival or even the disappearance of those passionate convictions which made civil war seem to the Middle Ages intrinsically worth while; but we cannot deny that life is made paler and that we are carried one step nearer to that state in which existence is seen as a vast emptiness which the imagination can no longer people with fascinating illusions.

For the more skeptical of the Victorians, love performed some of the functions of the God whom they had lost. Faced with it, many of even the most hard-headed turned, for the moment, mystical. They found themselves in the presence of something which awoke in them that sense of reverence which nothing else claimed, and something to which they felt, even in the very depths of their being, that an unquestioning loyalty was due. For them love, like God, demanded all sacrifices; but like Him, also, it rewarded the believer by investing all the phenomena of life with a meaning not yet analyzed away. We have grown used—more than they—to a Godless universe, but we are not yet accustomed to one which is loveless as well, and only when we have so become shall we realize what atheism really means.

The Tragic Fallacy

Through the legacy of their art the great ages have transmitted to us a dim image of their glorious vitality. When we turn the pages of a Sophoclean or a Shakespearean tragedy we participate faintly in the experience which created it and we sometimes presumptuously say that we "understand" the spirit of these works. But the truth is that we see them, even at best and in the moments when our souls expand most nearly to their dimensions, through a glass darkly.

It is so much easier to appreciate than to create that an age too feeble to reach the heights achieved by the members of a preceding one can still see those heights towering above its impotence, and so it is that, when we perceive a Sophocles or a Shakespeare soaring in an air which we can never hope to breathe, we say that we can "appreciate" them. But what we mean is that we are just able to wonder, and we can never hope to participate in the glorious vision of human life out of which they were created—not even to the extent of those humbler persons for whom they were written; for while to us the triumphant voices come from far away and tell of a heroic world which no longer exists, to them they spoke of immediate realities and revealed the inner meaning of events amidst which they still lived.

When the life has entirely gone out of a work of art come down to us from the past, when we read it without any emotional comprehension whatsoever and can no longer even imagine why the people for whom it was intended found it absorbing and satisfying, then, of course, it has ceased to be a work of art at all and has dwindled into one of those deceptive "documents" from which we get a false sense of comprehending through the intellect things which cannot be comprehended at all except by means of a kinship of feeling. And though all works from a past age have begun in this way to fade there are some, like the great Greek or Elizabethan tragedies, which are still halfway between the work of art and the document. They no longer can have for us the immediacy which they had for those to whom they originally belonged, but they have not yet eluded us entirely. We no longer live in the world which they represent, but we can half imagine it and we can measure the distance which we have moved away. We write no tragedies today, but we can still talk about the tragic spirit of which we would, perhaps, have no conception were it not for the works in question.

An age which could really "appreciate" Shakespeare or Sophocles would have something comparable to put beside them—something like them, not necessarily in form, or spirit, but at least in magnitude—some vision of life which would be, however different, equally ample and passionate. But when we move to put a modern masterpiece beside them, when we seek to compare them with, let us say, a *Ghosts* or a *Weavers,* we shrink as from the impulse to commit some folly and we feel as though we were about to superimpose Bowling Green upon the Great Prairies in order to ascertain which is the larger. The question, we see, is not primarily one of art but of the two worlds which two minds inhabited. No increased powers of expression, no greater gift for words, could have transformed Ibsen into Shakespeare. The materials out of which the latter created his works—his conception of human dignity, his sense of the importance of human passions, his vision of the amplitude of human life—simply did not and could not exist for Ibsen, as they did not and could not exist for his contemporaries. God and Man and Nature had all somehow dwindled in the course of the intervening centuries, not because the realistic creed of modern art led us to seek out mean people, but because this meanness of human life was somehow thrust upon us by the operation of that same process which led to the development of realistic theories of art by which our vision could be justified.

Hence, though we still apply, sometimes, the adjective "tragic" to one or another of those modern works of literature which describe human misery and which end more sadly even than they begin, the term is a misnomer since it is obvious that the works in question have nothing in common with the classical examples of the genre and produce in the reader a sense of depression which is the exact opposite of that elation generated when the spirit of a Shakespeare rises joyously superior to the outward calamities which he recounts and celebrates the greatness of the human spirit whose travail he describes. Tragedies, in that only sense of the word which has any distinctive meaning, are no longer written in either the dramatic or any other form, and the fact is not to be accounted for in any merely literary terms. It is not the result of any fashion in literature or of any deliberation to write about human nature or character under different aspects, any more than it is of either any greater sensitiveness of feeling which would make us shrink from the contemplation of the suffering of Medea or Othello or of any greater optimism which would make us more likely to see life in more cheerful terms. It is, on the contrary, the result of one of those enfeeblements of the human spirit not unlike that described in the previous chapter of this essay, and a further illustration of that gradual weakening of man's confidence in his ability to impose upon the phenomenon of life an interpretation acceptable to his desires which is the subject of the whole of the present discussion.

To explain that fact and to make clear how the creation of classical tragedy did consist in the successful effort to impose such a satisfactory interpretation will require, perhaps, the special section which follows, although the truth of the fact that it does impose such an interpretation must be evident to any one who has ever risen from the reading of *Oedipus* or *Lear* with that feeling of exultation which comes when we have been able, by rare good fortune, to enter into its spirit as completely as it is possible for us of a remoter and emotionally enfeebled age to enter it. Meanwhile one anticipatory remark may be ventured. If the plays and the novels of today deal with littler people and less mighty emotions it is not because we have become interested in commonplace souls and their unglamorous adventures but because we have come, willy-nilly, to see the soul of man as commonplace and its emotions as mean.

II

Tragedy, said Aristotle, is the "imitation of noble actions," and though it is some twenty-five hundred years since the dictum was uttered there is only one respect in which we are inclined to modify it. To us "imitation" seems a rather naïve word to apply to that process by which observation is turned into art, and we seek one which would define or at least imply the nature of that interposition of the personality of the artist between the object and the beholder which constitutes his function and by means of which he transmits a modified version, rather than a mere imitation, of the thing which he has contemplated.

In the search for this word the aestheticians of romanticism invented the term "expression" to describe the artistic purpose to which apparent imitation was subservient. Psychologists, on the other hand, feeling that the artistic process was primarily one by which reality is modified in such a way as to render it more acceptable to the desires of the artist, employed various terms in the effort to describe that distortion which the wish may produce in vision. And though many of the newer critics reject both romanticism and psychology, even they insist upon the fundamental fact that in art we are concerned, not with mere imitation but with the imposition of some form upon the material which it would not have if it were merely copied as a camera copies.

Tragedy is not, then, as Aristotle said, the *imitation* of noble actions, for, indeed, no one knows what a *noble* action is or whether or not such a thing as nobility exists in nature apart from the mind of man. Certainly the action of Achilles in dragging the dead body of Hector around the walls of Troy and under the eyes of Andromache, who had begged to be allowed to give it decent burial, is not to us a noble action, though it was such to Homer, who made it the subject of a noble passage in a noble poem. Certainly, too, the same action might conceivably be made the subject of a tragedy and the subject of a farce, depending upon the way in which it was treated; so that to say that tragedy is the *imitation* of a *noble* action is to be guilty of assuming, first, that art and photography are the same and, second, that there may be something inherently noble in an act as distinguished from the motives which prompted it or from the point of view from which it is regarded.

And yet, nevertheless, the idea of nobility is inseparable from the idea of tragedy, which cannot exist without it. If tragedy is not the imitation or even the modified representation of noble actions it is certainly a representation of actions *considered* as noble, and herein lies its essential nature, since no man can conceive it unless he is capable of believing in the great ness and importance of man. Its action is usually, if not always, calamitous, because it is only in calamity that the human spirit has the opportunity to reveal itself triumphant over the outward universe which fails to conquer it; but this calamity in tragedy is only a means to an end and the essential thing which distinguishes real tragedy from those distressing modern works sometimes called by its name is the fact that it is in the former alone that the artist has found himself capable of considering and of making us consider that his people and his actions have that amplitude and importance which make them noble. Tragedy arises then when, as in Periclean Greece or Elizabethan England, a people fully aware of the calamities of life is nevertheless serenely confident of the greatness of man, whose mighty passions and supreme fortitude are revealed when one of these calamities overtakes him.

To those who mistakenly think of it as something gloomy or depressing, who are incapable of recognizing the elation which its celebration of human greatness inspires, and who, therefore, confuse it with things merely miserable or pathetic, it must be a paradox that the happiest, most vigorous, and most confident ages which the world has ever known—the Periclean and the Elizabethan—should be exactly those which created and which most relished the mightiest tragedies; but the paradox is, of course, resolved by the fact that tragedy is essentially an expression, not of despair, but of the triumph over despair and of confidence in the value of human life. If Shakespeare himself ever had that "dark period" which his critics and biographers have imagined for him, it was at least no darkness like that bleak and arid despair which sometimes settles over modern spirits. In the midst of it he created both the elemental grandeur of Othello and the pensive majesty of Hamlet and, holding them up to his contemporaries, he said in the words of his own Miranda, "Oh, rare new world that hath *such* creatures in it."

All works of art which deserve their name have a happy end. This is indeed the thing which constitutes them art and through which they perform their function. Whatever the character of the events, fortunate or unfortunate, which they recount, they so mold or arrange or interpret them that we accept gladly the conclusion which they reach and would not have it otherwise. They may conduct us into the realm of pure fancy where wish and fact are identical and the world is remade exactly after the fashion of the heart's desire or they may yield some greater or less allegiance to fact; but they must always reconcile us in one way or another to the representation which they make and the distinctions between the genres are simply the distinctions between the means by which this reconciliation is effected.

Comedy laughs the minor mishaps of its characters away; drama solves all the difficulties which it allows to arise; and melodrama, separating good from evil by simple lines, distributes its rewards and punishments in accordance with the principles of a naïve justice which satisfies the simple souls of its audience, which are neither philosophical enough to question its primitive ethics nor critical enough to object to the way in which its neat events violate the laws of probability. Tragedy, the greatest and the most difficult of the arts, can adopt none of these methods; and yet it must reach its own happy end in its own way. Though its conclusion must be, by its premise, outwardly calamitous, though it must speak to those who know that the good man is cut off and that the fairest things are the first to perish, yet it must leave them, as *Othello* does, content that this is so. We must be and we are glad that Juliet dies and glad that Lear is turned out into the storm.

Milton set out, he said, to justify the ways of God to man, and his phrase, if it be interpreted broadly enough, may be taken as describing the function of all art, which must, in some way or other, make the life which it seems to represent satisfactory to those who see its reflection in the magic mirror, and it must gratify or at least reconcile the desires of the beholder, not necessarily, as the naïver exponents of Freudian psychology maintain, by gratifying individual and often eccentric wishes, but at least by satisfying the universally human desire to find in the world some justice, some meaning, or, at the very least, some recognizable order. Hence it is that every real tragedy, however tremendous it may be, is an affirmation of faith in life, a declaration that even if God is not in his Heaven, then at least Man is in his world.

We accept gladly the outward defeats which it describes for the sake of the inward victories which it reveals. Juliet died, but not before she had shown how great and resplendent a thing love could be; Othello plunged the dagger into his own breast, but not before he had revealed that greatness of soul which makes his death seem unimportant. Had he died in the instant when he struck the blow, had he perished still believing that the world was as completely black as he saw it before the innocence of Desdemona was revealed to him, then, for him at least, the world would have been merely damnable, but Shakespeare kept him alive long enough to allow him to learn his error and hence to die, not in despair, but in the full acceptance of the tragic reconciliation to life. Perhaps it would be pleasanter if men could believe what the child is taught —that the good are happy and that things turn out as they should—but it is far more important to be able to believe, as Shakespeare did, that however much things in the outward world may go awry, man has, nevertheless, splendors of his own and that, in a word, Love and Honor and Glory are not words but realities.

Thus for the great ages tragedy is not an expression of despair but the means by which they saved themselves from it. It is a profession of faith, and a sort of religion; a way of looking at life by virtue of which it is robbed of its pain. The sturdy soul of the tragic author seizes upon suffering and uses it only as a means by which joy may be wrung out of existence, but it is not to be forgotten that he is enabled to do so only because of his belief in the greatness of human nature and because, though he has lost the child's faith in life, he has not lost his far more important faith in human nature. A tragic writer does not have to believe in God, but he must believe in man.

And if, then, the Tragic Spirit is in reality the product of a religious faith in which, sometimes at least, faith in the greatness of God is replaced by faith in the greatness of man, it serves, of course, to perform the function of religion, to make life tolerable for those who participate in its beneficent illusion. It purges the souls of those who might otherwise despair and it makes endurable the realization that the events of the outward world do not correspond with the desires of the heart, and thus, in its own particular way, it does what all religions do, for it gives a rationality, a meaning, and a justification to the universe. But if it has the strength it has also the weakness of all faiths, since it may—nay, it must—be ultimately lost as reality, encroaching further and further into the realm of imagination, leaving less and less room in which that imagination can build its refuge.

III

It is, indeed, only at a certain stage in the development of the realistic intelligence of a people that the tragic faith can exist. A naïver people may have, as the ancient men of the north had, a body of legends which are essentially tragic, or it may have only (and need only) its happy and childlike mythology which arrives inevitably at its happy end, where the only ones who suffer "deserve" to do so and in which, therefore, life is represented as directly and easily acceptable. A too sophisticated society on the other hand—one which, like ours, has outgrown not merely the simple optimism of the child but also that vigorous, one might almost say adolescent, faith in the nobility of man which marks a Sophocles or a Shakespeare—has neither fairy tales to assure it that all is always right in the end nor tragedies to make it believe that it rises superior in soul to the outward calamities which befall it.

Distrusting its thought, despising its passions, realizing its impotent unimportance in the universe, it can tell itself no stories except those which make it still more acutely aware of its trivial miseries. When its heroes (sad misnomer for the pitiful creatures who people contemporary fiction) are struck down it is not, like Oedipus, by the gods that they are struck but only, like Oswald Alving, by syphilis, for they know that the gods, even if they existed, would not trouble with them, and they cannot attribute to themselves in art an importance in which they do not believe. Their so-called tragedies do not and cannot end with one of those splendid calamities which in Shakespeare seem to reverberate through the universe, because they cannot believe that the universe trembles when their love is, like Romeo's, cut off or when the place where they (small as they are) have gathered up their trivial treasure is, like Othello's sanctuary, defiled. Instead, mean misery piles on mean misery, petty misfortune follows petty misfortune, and despair becomes intolerable because it is no longer even significant or important.

Ibsen once made one of his characters say that he did not read much because he found reading "irrelevant," and the adjective was brilliantly chosen because it held implications even beyond those of which Ibsen was consciously aware. What is it that made the classics irrelevant to him and to us? Is it not just exactly those to him impossible premises which make tragedy what it is, those assumptions that the soul of man is great, that the universe (together with whatever gods may be) concerns itself with him and that he is, in a word, noble? Ibsen turned to village politics for exactly the same reason that his contemporaries and his successors have, each in his own way, sought out some aspect of the common man and his common life—because, that is to say, here was at least something small enough for him to be able to believe.

Bearing this fact in mind, let us compare a modern "tragedy" with one of the great works of a happy age, not in order to judge of their relative technical merits but in order to determine to what extent the former deserves its name by achieving a tragic solution capable of purging the soul or of reconciling the emotions to the life which it pictures. And in order to make the comparison as fruitful as possible let us choose *Hamlet* on the one hand and on the other a play like *Ghosts* which was not only written by perhaps the most powerful as well as the most typical of modern writers but which is, in addition, the one of his works which seems most nearly to escape that triviality which cannot be entirely escaped by anyone who feels, as all contemporary minds do, that man is relatively trivial.

In *Hamlet* a prince ("in understanding, how like a god!") has thrust upon him from the unseen world a duty to redress a wrong which concerns not merely him, his mother, and his uncle, but the moral order of the universe. Erasing all trivial fond records from his mind, abandoning at once both his studies and his romance because it has been his good fortune to be called upon to take part in an action of cosmic importance, he plunges (at first) not into action but into thought, weighing the claims which are made upon him and contemplating the grandiose complexities of the universe. And when the time comes at last for him to die he dies, not as a failure, but as a success. Not only has the universe regained the balance which had been upset by what *seemed* the monstrous crime of the guilty pair ("there is nothing either good nor ill but thinking makes it so"), but in the process by which that readjustment is made a mighty mind has been given the opportunity, first to contemplate the magnificent scheme of which it is a part and then to demonstrate the greatness of its spirit by playing a rôle in the grand style which it called for. We do not need to despair in *such* a world if it has *such* creatures in it.

Turn now to *Ghosts*—look upon this picture and upon that. A young man has inherited syphilis from his father. Struck by a to him mysterious malady he returns to his northern village, learns the hopeless truth about himself, and persuades his mother to poison him. The incidents prove, perhaps, that pastors should not endeavor to keep a husband and wife together unless they know what they are doing. But what a world is this in which a great writer can deduce nothing more than that from his greatest work and how are we to be purged or reconciled when we see it acted? Not only is the failure utter, but it is trivial and meaningless as well.

Yet the journey from Elsinore to Skien is precisely the journey which the human spirit has made, exchanging in the process princes for invalids and gods for disease. We say, as Ibsen would say, that the problems of Oswald Alving are more "relevant" to our life than the problems of Hamlet, that the play in which he appears is more "real" than the other more glamorous one, but it is exactly because we find it so that we are condemned. We can believe in Oswald but we cannot believe in Hamlet, and a light has gone out in the universe. Shakespeare justifies the ways of God to man, but in Ibsen there is no such happy end and with him tragedy, so called, has become merely an expression of our despair at finding that such justification is no longer possible.

Modern critics have sometimes been puzzled to account for the fact that the concern of ancient tragedy is almost exclusively with kings and courts. They have been tempted to accuse even Aristotle of a certain naïveté in assuming (as he seems to assume) that the "nobility" of which he speaks as necessary to a tragedy implies a nobility of rank as well as of soul, and they have sometimes regretted that Shakespeare did not devote himself more than he did to the serious consideration of those common woes of the common man which subsequent writers have exploited with increasing pertinacity. Yet the tendency to lay the scene of a tragedy at the court of a king is not the result of any arbitrary convention but of the fact that the tragic writers believed easily in greatness just as we believe easily in meanness. To Shakespeare, robes and crowns and jewels are the garments most appropriate to man because they are the fitting outward manifestation of his inward majesty, but to us they seem absurd because the man who bears them has, in our estimation, so pitifully shrunk. We do not write about kings because we do not believe that any man is worthy to be one and we do not write about courts because hovels seem to us to be dwellings more appropriate to the creatures who inhabit them. Any modern attempt to dress characters in robes ends only by making us aware of a comic incongruity and any modern attempt to furnish them with a language resplendent like Shakespeare's ends only in bombast.

True tragedy capable of performing its function and of purging the soul by reconciling man to his woes can exist only by virtue of a certain pathetic fallacy far more inclusive than that to which the name is commonly given. The romantics, feeble descendants of the tragic writers to whom they are linked by their effort to see life and nature in grandiose terms, loved to imagine that the sea or the sky had a way of according itself with their moods, of storming when they stormed and smiling when they smiled. But the tragic spirit sustains itself by an assumption much more far-reaching and no more justified. Man as it sees him lives in a world which he may not dominate but which is always aware of him. Occupying the exact center of a universe which would have no meaning except for him and being so little below the angels that, if he believes in God, he has no hesitation in imagining Him formed as he is formed and crowned with a crown like that which he or one of his fellows wears, he assumes that each of his acts reverberates through the universe. His passions are important to him because he believes them important throughout all time and all space; the very fact that he can sin (no modern can) means that this universe is watching his acts; and though he may perish, a God leans out from infinity to strike him down. And it is exactly because an Ibsen cannot think of man in any such terms as these that his persons have so shrunk and that his "tragedy" has lost that power which real tragedy always has of making that infinitely ambitious creature called man content to accept his misery if only he can be made to feel great enough and important enough. An Oswald is not a Hamlet chiefly because he has lost that tie with the natural and supernatural world which the latter had. No ghost will leave the other world to warn or encourage him, there is no virtue and no vice which he can possibly have which can be really important, and when he dies neither his death nor the manner of it will be, outside the circle of two or three people as unnecessary as himself, any more important than that of a rat behind the arras.

Perhaps we may dub the illusion upon which the tragic spirit is nourished the Tragic, as opposed to the Pathetic, Fallacy, but fallacy though it is, upon its existence depends not merely the writing of tragedy but the existence of that religious feeling of which tragedy is an expression and by means of which a people aware of the dissonances of life manages nevertheless to hear them as harmony. Without it neither man nor his passions can seem great enough or important enough to justify the sufferings which they entail, and literature, expressing the mood of a people, begins to despair where once it had exulted. Like the belief in love and like most of the other mighty illusions by means of which human life has been given a value, the Tragic Fallacy depends ultimately upon the assumption which man so readily makes that something outside his own being, some "spirit not himself"—be it God, Nature, or that still vaguer thing called a Moral Order—joins him in the emphasis which he places upon this or that and confirms him in his feeling that his passions and his opinions are important. When his instinctive faith in that correspondence between the outer and the inner world fades, his grasp upon the faith that sustained him fades also, and Love or Tragedy or what not ceases to be the reality which it was because he is never strong enough in his own insignificant self to stand alone in a universe which snubs him with its indifference.

In both the modern and the ancient worlds tragedy was dead long before writers were aware of the fact. Seneca wrote his frigid melodramas under the impression that he was following in the footsteps of Sophocles, and Dryden probably thought that his *All for Love* was an improvement upon Shakespeare, but in time we awoke to the fact that no amount of rhetorical bombast could conceal the fact that grandeur was not to be counterfeited when the belief in its possibility was dead, and turning from the hero to the common man we inaugurated the era of realism. For us no choice remains except that between mere rhetoric and the frank consideration of our fellow men, who may be the highest of the anthropoids but who are certainly too far below the angels to imagine either that these angels can concern themselves with them or that they can catch any glimpse of even the soles of angelic feet. We can no longer tell tales of the fall of noble men because we do not believe that noble men exist. The best that we can achieve is pathos and the most that we can do is to feel sorry for ourselves. Man has put off his royal robes and it is only in sceptered pomp that tragedy can come sweeping by.

IV

Neitzsche was the last of the great philosophers to attempt a tragic justification of life. His central and famous dogma—"Life is good *because* it is painful"— sums up in a few words the desperate and almost meaningless paradox to which he was driven in his effort to reduce to rational terms the far more imaginative conception which is everywhere present but everywhere unanalyzed in a Sophocles or a Shakespeare and by means of which they rise triumphant over the manifold miseries of life. But the very fact that Nietzsche could not even attempt to state in any except intellectual terms an attitude which is primarily unintellectual and to which, indeed, intellectual analysis is inevitably fatal is proof of the distance which he had been carried (by the rationalizing tendencies of the human mind) from the possibility of the tragic solution which he sought; and the confused, half-insane violence of his work will reveal, by the contrast which it affords with the serenity of the tragic writers whom he admired, how great was his failure.

Fundamentally this failure was, moreover, conditioned by exactly the same thing which has conditioned the failure of all modern attempts to achieve what he attempted—by the fact, that is to say, that tragedy must have a hero if it is not to be merely an accusation against, instead of a justification of, the world in which it occurs. Tragedy is, as Aristotle said, an imitation of noble actions, and Nietzsche, for all his enthusiasm for the Greek tragic writers, was palsied by the universally modern incapacity to conceive man as noble. Out of this dilemma, out of his need to find a hero who could give to life as he saw it the only possible justification, was born the idea of the Superman, but the Superman is, after all, only a hypothetical being, destined to become what man actually was in the eyes of the great tragic writers—a creature (as Hamlet said) "how infinite in capacities, in understanding how like a god." Thus Nietzsche lived half in the past through his literary enthusiasms and half in the future through his grandiose dreams, but for all his professed determination to justify existence he was no more able than the rest of us to find the present acceptable. Life, he said in effect, is not a Tragedy now but perhaps it will be when the Ape-man has been transformed into a hero (the *Übermensch*), and trying to find that sufficient, he went mad.

He failed, as all moderns must fail when they attempt, like him, to embrace the tragic spirit as a religious faith, because the resurgence of that faith is not an intellectual but a vital phenomenon, something not achieved by taking thought but born, on the contrary, out of an instinctive confidence in life which is nearer to the animal's unquestioning allegiance to the scheme of nature than it is to that critical intelligence characteristic of a fully developed humanism. And like other faiths it is not to be recaptured merely by reaching an intellectual conviction that it would be desirable to do so.

Modern psychology has discovered (or at least strongly emphasized) the fact that under certain conditions desire produces belief, and having discovered also that the more primitive a given mentality the more completely are its opinions determined by its wishes, modern psychology has concluded that the best mind is that which most resists the tendency to believe a thing simply because it would be pleasant or advantageous to do so. But justified as this conclusion may be from the intellectual point of view, it fails to take into account the fact that in a universe as badly adapted as this one to human as distinguished from animal needs, this ability to will a belief may bestow an enormous vital advantage as it did, for instance, in the case at present under discussion where it made possible for Shakespeare the compensations of a tragic faith completely inaccessible to Nietzsche. Pure intelligence, incapable of being influenced by desire and therefore also incapable of choosing one opinion rather than another simply because the one chosen is the more fruitful or beneficent, is doubtless a relatively perfect instrument for the pursuit of truth, but the question (likely, it would seem, to be answered in the negative) is simply whether or not the spirit of man can endure the literal and inhuman truth.

Certain ages and simple people have conceived of the action which passes upon the stage of the universe as of something in the nature of a Divine Comedy, as something, that is to say, which will reach its end with the words "and they lived happily ever after." Others, less naïve and therefore more aware of those maladjustments whose reality, at least so far as outward events are concerned, they could not escape, have imposed upon it another artistic form and called it a Divine Tragedy, accepting its catastrophe as we accept the catastrophe of an *Othello,* because of its grandeur. But a Tragedy, Divine or otherwise, must, it may again be repeated, have a hero, and from the universe as we see it both the Glory of God and the Glory of Man have departed. Our cosmos may be farcical or it may be pathetic but it has not the dignity of tragedy and we cannot accept it as such.

Yet our need for the consolations of tragedy has not passed with the passing of our ability to conceive it. Indeed, the dissonances which it was tragedy's function to resolve grow more insistent instead of diminishing. Our passions, our disappointments, and our sufferings remain important to us though important to nothing else and they thrust themselves upon us with an urgency which makes it impossible for us to dismiss them as the mere trivialities which, so our intellects tell us, they are. And yet, in the absence of tragic faith or the possibility of achieving it, we have no way in which we may succeed in giving them the dignity which would not only render them tolerable but transform them as they were transformed by the great ages into joys. The death of tragedy is, like the death of love, one of those emotional fatalities as the result of which the human as distinguished from the natural world grows more and more a desert.

Poetry, said Santayana in his famous phrase, is "religion which is no longer believed," but it depends, nevertheless, upon its power to revive in us a sort of temporary or provisional credence and the nearer it can come to producing an illusion of belief the greater is its power as poetry. Once the Tragic Spirit was a living faith and out of it tragedies were written. Today these great expressions of a great faith have declined, not merely into poetry, but into a kind of poetry whose premises are so far from any we can really accept that we can only partially and dimly grasp its meaning.

We read but we do not write tragedies. The tragic solution of the problem of existence, the reconciliation to life by means of the tragic spirit is, that is to say, now only a fiction surviving in art. When that art itself has become, as it probably will, completely meaningless, when we have ceased not only to write but to *read* tragic works, then it will be lost and in all real senses forgotten, since the devolution from Religion to Art to Document will be complete.

SIX

Life, Art, and Peace

In the opinion of the theologians of the Middle Age the conduct of life had been reduced to the status of an exact science. The end to be achieved—salvation of the soul—was definitely fixed and the general principles to be followed were clearly understood. They accepted the Laws of God in a fashion exactly parallel to that in which the contemporary scientist accepts the Laws of Nature, and they no more doubted certain fundamental principles like the forgiveness of sins than one of these modern scientists doubts the principle of the conservation of energy. Hence they could proceed as he does to devise and to describe the means by which these principles could be taken advantage of in order to secure a desired end.

They sometimes spoke of these central dogmas as mysteries but they were mysterious only in the sense that electricity is mysterious, for though they might, like electricity, contain intimate secrets and spring from ultimate causes which no man could understand, yet one knew that they would operate in a certain way and that they could be counted upon to do so. No man knows whence the wind cometh nor whither it bloweth but that, said an American skeptic, makes very little difference since we know exactly how it behaves when it gets here, and his rationalistic hardheadedness was not unlike the theological hardheadedness of certain learned doctors who rebuked the prying curiosity of those who proposed too many whys and wherefores when they should be taking practical advantage of the laws which God had instituted and revealed in order that a knowledge of their unchanging *modus operandi* might be used.

Grace could be piped, like oil, from its copious fountainhead; the current flowing out from God could be conducted from priest to priest on to the ultimate consumer, just as electricity is conducted through electrically connected wires; and holy water could be used to destroy evil spirits both as surely and, in one sense, as unmysteriously as carbolic acid kills germs. Woe to him, but to him only, who was ignorant of the laws of God or who perversely refused to live in accordance with the rules of spiritual health!

Disease could be cured and disease could also, in considerable measure, be prevented. There were desperate surgical operations performed when the sinner far gone in sin made a deathbed confession and was saved for eternal life by having his spiritual cancers cut away; there were stern but healthful regimens imposed when incipient damnation was arrested by a course of systematic penance; and there were, besides, rules for rational living by which health might be maintained. The conduct of life was a science, or perhaps it would be better to say that it was, for the layman at least, a technique. Theologians, like scientists, might investigate to extend the knowledge of the laws according to which the universe worked, but the ordinary man accepted what he was told and used their knowledge by employing their inventions and applying whatever he knew to the solution of his individual problem. There were great scientific monographs for the learned, no more understandable to the common man of the Middle Age than the writings of Michelson or Clerk-Maxwell are understandable to the common man of today, but there were also popular "outlines" to instruct or amuse him and practical little handbooks enabling him to care for his soul as a modern man regulates his own diet when he finds himself getting too fat or keeps his radio set functioning at its highest efficiency.

In those days, then, men approached the problem of ordering their inward lives in the same practical spirit in which we approach that of ordering our material conditions. There were, in a word, rules to live by, and, theoretically at least, the conduct of life never involved questions any more fundamental than those concerned with the practical application of known principles to specific situations. On certain occasions one appealed to the Virgin, on others to St. Christopher or St. Anthony; one consulted a priest, and, following his advice, one prayed or one fasted. Nor does, indeed, this view of the "good life" necessarily disappear as long as a legalistic religion, like that which the disciples of Christ erected upon the Hebraic foundation, continues to exist.

One may find it very clearly expressed, for example, in a little allegory written by the poet Cowper, who may be taken as a representative of Protestantism in its most completely logical form. God, says Cowper, is the hospitable master of a magnificent mansion which He has erected for the entertainment of guests. There is one road which leads directly to it, that road is plainly marked, and it is surely not the Master's fault if some travelers refuse to take it or if they stop to argue either that some other road will do just as well or that He ought to have made it accessible from various directions. To lead the good life, to make existence a success, one needs nothing except the wit to read the plain sign and the common sense to choose the road thus plainly marked.

But the ability to accept a plan of life so delightfully simple depends both upon a complete confidence in the dogmas of some given religion and also upon the fact that the aim of existence is fixed for us by such a religion—that we know, in a word, why we are here and to what purpose we ought to devote our lives. As soon as one begins to doubt either the validity of the laws of God considered as the fundamental principles of a science which happens to be called theology, or as soon as one begins to raise a question as to the purpose of life, then the problem of conducting that life ceases to be merely a problem of technique and begins to involve certain ultimate questions concerning the end which we wish to reach or concerning what may properly be called success in life.

In practice such questions actually arise as soon as any given religion begins to become a formal instead of a living system of beliefs, as soon as a people, while continuing to agree as a matter of form that the purpose of life is preparation for eternity, begins nevertheless to seek purely temporal ends. And this means, of course, that the questions actually existed for a great many people even during those ages called ages of faith and that they were of primary importance to most people in the time, let us say, of the poet Cowper, since most people, then as now, *acted* as though there were ends to be achieved in this life, however much they might profess a formal belief in the Christian doctrine which teaches them that it is meaningless except as a preparation for eternity. Yet the questions become more and more acute and the efforts to solve them more and more conscious as people cease more and more even to pretend to believe that they live primarily "to save their souls." Even the formal assumption that the conduct of life is the subject of an established science from whose general principles practical rules for the successful regulation of everyday acts may be logically deduced becomes impossible, since we no longer agree that we know just in what the success we hope to obtain would consist.

Hence arises a multiplication of philosophies and the formulation of innumerable definitions of the "good life" which range all the way from that implied in Nietzsche's "live dangerously" to that implied in various catchwords like the characteristically American nebulosity "service," whose very multiplicity reveals how far mankind has drifted from the possibility of formulating any generally accepted rationalization to impose upon those vital impulses which lead them to live and how far they are, therefore, from the possibility of regarding life as a science. A few years ago, however, some one let fall the phrase, "Life is an art." It was given a wide circulation in Havelock Ellis's essay *The Dance of Life* and among members of the intellectual class it sprang into an immediate popularity which revealed, not only how much that class felt the need of defining some attitude from which the subject of the conduct of life could be approached, but also—since science and art are the two members of a conventional dualism—how completely it had abandoned any belief in the possibility that life could have any purpose fixed in the ultimate nature of things as the result of which its fruitful employment might be made the subject of a science.

Now the aims of art have never been clearly defined. The ends which individual works of art attempt to achieve are, in appearance at least, diverse, and the means which it employs seem almost infinitely variable. Hence it is that to say that life is an art and to use that term "art" in contradistinction to science seems to provide a greater latitude in the choice of both its aims and its methods than could possibly be permitted by a moralist or a theologian who regarded it as a science, and it may very well be that this vagueness which, in spite of all the volumes which have been written on the subject of aesthetics, still surrounds the word "art," may constitute the chief reason for the widespread use of the phrase by people unable to formulate for themselves any definition of the purpose of life as clear and as simple as that offered by either a Roman Catholic theologian or a logical Protestant.

And yet, whatever its ultimate meaning may be, and whether or not it can be shown to have any precise signification, the popularity of this saying that "life is an art" implies something which cannot but be important for the understanding of the modern temper, since only a modern could formulate the phrase. It is to the effort to seek out that meaning and to discover what are the limitations of life considered as material for the creation of a work of art that the present section of this essay will be devoted. What is art and how may its principles be applied to the conduct of life?

II

In one sense the aim of the scientist and the aim of the artist are the same since both are in pursuit of what they call truth; but the difference between them may be said to consist in this, that while for science there is only one Truth, for the artist there are many. The scientist, that is to say, is in search of truths which owe their name to the fact that they correspond to something in the world outside himself, while the artist is in search of those which need to be true only in the sense that they seem true to him and that they hold good within the artificial universe which is inclosed within the frame of the work of art he is creating.

The scientist must submit to the judgment of others, not merely the conclusions which he reaches but also the premises with which he began and the methods which he uses in developing his work from them; but the artist, within very wide limits at least, is allowed to choose whatever premises he likes and, as a result, it is by no means necessary that all good artists should agree to anything like the same extent that all good scientists must agree. In recognition of this fact literary critics never tire of asserting as a fundamental principle cf criticism that in discussing a work of art we must concern ourselves exclusively with the question, "How far did the artist succeed in doing what he set out to do or in saying what he set out to say?" and never with the question of whether we consider his purpose useless or pernicious. To do so would be, they say, to introduce moral or other extraneous questions into the realm of aesthetics, and from this we may conclude that if life is an art, then an analogous principle must be accepted as the basis of all efforts to criticize it.

The first effect of a determination to regard life as an art instead of as a science would, then, seem necessarily to be to grant to the individual a much greater latitude than the theologian would allow him in choosing the purpose to which he wishes to devote his life and would lead us to judge of his success, not by considering the end which he proposes but merely by the extent to which he is successful in his effort to achieve that end. It would be to assume (as the modern man feels almost compelled to assume) that life has no purpose fixed by a power outside of life (as distinguished from such purpose as the individual may be able to choose or believe in for himself) and hence to assume also that there is no more any such thing as *the* good life than there is any such thing as *the* good work of art, although, of course, there may be various good lives just as there are various good works of art.

When considered from such a point of view the treatises on morality on which the theologian lays so much stress would seem to bear about the same relation to the art of life as treatises on rhetoric bear to the art of letters, and to be scarcely more useful. Both are based on the assumption that the subject with which they deal is a science governed by certain fixed laws and aiming at fixed ends, and both assume also that the methods of one successful practitioner of either life or letters may be formulated for the imitation of those who aspire to a similar success. But the good writer does not usually learn much from such textbooks. He generally discovers that he is able by their aid to produce nothing but frigid rhetorical exercises and that he must create his own original style if he is to achieve any real success. This is the natural result of the fact that literature is an art instead of a science, that it depends, that is to say, too much on the individual personality to be reducible to a teachable technique, and it serves to explain by analogy why moral treatises offer so little aid to the individual in search of a good life. The principles there laid down may possibly be those which a certain man followed in achieving a certain kind of success in a certain kind of life but they may be as useless to another man as the rhetorical analysis of a classical writer's sentence structure is to another writer. Rhetoric takes no real account of the art in literature and morality takes no account of the art in life.

Perhaps, however, the exact thing here meant can more easily be made clear by means of an example taken from the creative writing of a man who did, at least at certain times, attempt to regard life as an art, and for that purpose a passage may be chosen from one of the novels of Henry James. Those who have read *The American* will remember that toward the end of that work the hero turns into a little church to meditate on the wrongs which have been inflicted on him and that though at first he considers the possibility of revenge, of retaliating on those who have injured him, yet after a little he repudiates the idea because, says James, he came to realize that "revenge was not his game."

Now the thing to be noticed here is the fact that

this typical though early Jamesian hero did not conclude that revenge was "wrong," that an obligation
to eschew it was imposed upon him from without or
that there was any science of life from whose principles the folly of revenge could be deduced, but only
that such revenge "was not his game." He had, in
other words, adopted a certain style of living and
acting, exactly as an artist adopts a certain style for
the execution of a work of art, and he realized that
an act of revenge was inappropriate to that style, exactly as an artist might realize that a certain incident
or observation or shape was not appropriate to the
particular work in hand. He did not, be it further
observed, say that revenge was not, or ought not be,
anybody's "game," for, by implication at least, he
recognized the fact that other artists working in other
styles might, on the other hand, find it the only appropriate thing—that Benvenuto Cellini, for example,
would fail if he refused to take a revenge just as surely
as the hero here under discussion would fail if he consented to do so, since revenge was as distinctly a part
of Benvenuto's "game" as it was distinctly not a part
of his.

To him life was, in other words, an art, and in
art all styles are good provided that they are consistent
and harmonious within themselves. There is the
"style" of Benvenuto Cellini and there is the "style"
of St. Francis of Assisi, both of whom led successful
lives because each of them lived in accordance with
the law of his being. The science of morals endeavors
to divide men into the good and the bad by determining whether or not their purposes and their deeds
accord with certain fixed principles and rules established outside themselves, but aesthetics can only pretend to judge them in accordance with their failure
or success in developing themselves according to their
self-chosen style. It cannot recognize the existence of

good or bad men but only of successful or unsuccessful artists. Life has its heroes and its villains, its soubrettes and its ingénues, and all rôles may be acted well.

Thus, though the popularity of the saying that life is an art is subsequent to the career of Henry James as a novelist, he had, nevertheless, so fallen into the habit of thinking of it as such that one may find in his work very convenient illustrations of the first and most immediate effects of such an attitude. The Puritanism which he inherited and which determined so many of his most fundamental instincts was sufficient to guarantee him against the possibility of following this line of thought out to its logical nihilistic conclusion, and there were kinds of lives as well as of art which—happily perhaps—he had not sufficient catholicity of taste to appreciate; but having outgrown the "scientific morality" of his Puritan ancestors, he was endeavoring to replace it with an aesthetic attitude which would give him that basis for making distinctions which is necessary not only for the novelist but also for every man who makes an effort to live humanly in the natural universe.

He was, however, careful never to treat in his novels any except decorous people, people who, however emancipated they might think themselves from moral principles, did nevertheless always conduct themselves in such a way as to keep within the limits of a certain propriety. He never chose to describe any of those terrifying "artists" who, like the great criminals, the great conquerors, or even like Benvenuto himself, live quite "successfully" because quite consistently in accordance with the style which they have chosen, and he did not do so because he realized, consciously or unconsciously, that those moral instincts which were still strong within him would not permit him to give an aesthetic justification to any manner of life which violated too strongly the moral principles which survived in him in a form still capable of producing very intense repugnances.

James, then, considered that life is an art, but he never dared to test his theory outside the walls of a drawing-room, and though this timid compromise, this constant hesitation between a thoroughgoing aestheticism and an attenuated Puritan morality, served the purpose of a novelist who confined his attention to a very quiet scene, it is difficult to see how the philosopher who proposes to consider existence as a whole from an aesthetic standpoint can avoid a far bolder application of aesthetic principles.

Considered as artistic creations, Hamlet and Othello are no greater and therefore no better than Macbeth or Iago. In the tragedy, villain and hero are equal, and if the meaning of existence is an artistic meaning, then the same is true in life also. The life led by the great monster is as truly the good life as that led by the great saint. Man has the liberty of choosing what James called the "game" he will play (i.e., the style to be adopted in that work of art which is his life) and the liberty of choice cannot be limited anywhere by any except aesthetic considerations without introducing the idea of morality, which, if it is intellectually justifiable at one point is intellectually justifiable at others. Life being an art and not a science, we may become either Cellini or St. Francis; but if that is true we may also become Napoleon or the Marquis de Sade. Both of the latter played rôles in that Tragedy or Comedy or Farce called the history of the world, both played well enough to be remembered as classical examples of how "their game" might successfully be played, and hence both were greater artists than the thousands whom morality would judge far more favorably.

In the graphic arts shadows are no less important than high lights, and in the literary arts villains are

no less important than heroes. We do not praise one
and blame the other, we do not say that it is better
to be a spot of sun than the shadow of a tree, and in
the world where life is an art Good and Evil are only
the names of high light and shadow. Nor is such
thoroughgoing aestheticism anything at all new in
the world, since it was indeed exactly the philosophy
formulated by certain Gnostic sects whose creed was
the result of the operation of the subtle intellect of
the classical world upon the naïvely vital religion of
the Christians and to whom we may turn in order to
find what are the ultimate logical conclusions to be
drawn from the proposition that life is an art.

III

These Gnostics had set out upon the perilous enter-
prise called thinking with the avowed purpose of solv-
ing the problem of evil. They had accepted the proposition which all men, led by their wish, naturally
accept—the proposition, that is to say, that God is
good—and they felt the need to reconcile it with the
evil and suffering which they saw everywhere around
them. Since this evil was copious and omnipresent it
must, they thought, serve some useful purpose and
be, that is to say, not really evil but merely a different
kind of good. They were not blessed with that
naïveté which permitted the ordinary Christian to reconcile the omnipotent benevolence of God with the
existence of a Devil, since they were logical enough to
see that a God who permitted the existence of such an
evil power would have to be either not all benevolent
or not all powerful, but they did nevertheless devise
an explanation quite worthy of the artistic subtlety of
the Greek mind.

The Good, they said, is like everything else an Idea,
and the various virtues—Benevolence, Justice, Purity,
and what not—can exist only as Ideas perceived or
entertained by the mind. But the mind, it must be re-

membered, cannot realize the existence of anything unless its opposite exists also. We would, for example, have no word for and therefore no Idea of light if we did not know what darkness is, and similarly the Idea of purity could not exist without the Idea of impurity by means of which it is defined. In a world where everybody was always and equally just or kind, neither Justice nor Kindness would exist in the mind, and hence evils of all kinds are permitted in order that their corresponding goods may exist. The cruel man, for instance, is not only tolerated but encouraged because his cruelty serves no less than the kindness of another to make real the Idea of kindness in that consciousness where alone the realest reality can exist.

This solution of the problem of evil was not only extremely subtle but based upon quite artistic principles since it not only regarded human character from the standpoint of those who would require of a man only that he play his rôle, villainous or heroic, in a manner suitable to the part he had undertaken, but also viewed the whole universe as a species of drama into which God had introduced evil and suffering in exactly the same way in which a playwright introduces them into his play—for the purpose, that is to say, of contrast. Seen from such an angle God becomes an impresario-playwright and man an actor, or, to change the metaphor, the universe is a great painting in which those shadows called evil are no less important or admirable than those high lights called good.

But however consistent this point of view may be, it led the Gnostics to the consideration of certain paradoxical propositions which they, with resolute logic, hastened to embrace. If the evil man is no less necessary than the good, why should we withhold from him our admiration and approval any more than we withhold our applause from that artist (often the most distinguished of the company) who enacts the villain in the play? Abel was good but so was Cain.

and if, grown bold, we approach now the central mystery of our religion, what of Christ and of Judas? Without Judas there would have been no crucifixion, and without the crucifixion there would have been no salvation. Jesus the Savior had need of the Traitor without whom He would have been powerless to save, and hence we owe our redemption no less to Judas than to Him. Christ, to be sure, said that it would have been better for Judas had he never been born, and so be it. But it would surely not have been better for us. Let us, then, canonize St. Judas, putting him whose soul was damned in order that we might be saved at least as high as that other Savior whose happier fate it was to pass from the Cross to eternal glory. And so they did.

The logic is admirable. It is doubtless, however, hardly necessary to add that these intellectual paradoxes led to examples of conduct which might be easily justified by Gnostic theology but which were not only highly scandalous in the eyes of less "artistic" sects but actually destructive of social order which was replaced by anarchy. The Gnostics knew how to think very subtly indeed and they furnished more than one *mauvais quart d'heure* to the orthodox Fathers who responded to them at length, but they did not know how to live in a world where many things work better in social practice than logic does.

It is rather difficult to carry on trade with a man who may be planning to revivify your Idea of justice by cheating you unmercifully, and rather difficult successfully to bring up a family when the father illustrates benevolence indirectly by beating the children or when the mother sets out to secure a clear Idea of purity by prostituting all of her daughters. And so it is that the Gnostics faded out of history by a process which seems never to have been chronicled but which it is not difficult to imagine, leaving the world to those people who did not think life an art, who had supreme confidence in a "science" of morality which was often fantastically arbitrary and completely indefensible from any intellectual standpoint but which did, nevertheless, by virtue of the mere fact that it was generally accepted, give a stability to a society in which at least man-the-animal could live and perpetuate his species.

This brand of Gnosticism was not, then, a very practical philosophy of life, and yet it is to it or to something very much like it that one must turn if one would discover the full implication of the saying that life is an art, since one finds in Henry James, for example, only a timid and very restricted effort to apply the principle and since the majority of those who have turned hopefully to the examination of the saying have done so merely because they saw in it the possibility of something which would replace discarded moral codes by a workable philosophy of life allowing a slightly greater latitude for the differing needs of the various individuals whose first need, now that authority has failed, must be to discover what, for them, would be either *the* good life or, at least, *a* good life.

Yet it is not to be supposed that no moderns have followed out to the end the implications of this aesthetic attitude. One might, for example, cite the case of Ernest Renan whose profound knowledge of early Christian thought no doubt influenced his own thinking and who once delivered himself of the following opinion: "The universe," he said, "is a spectacle which the Good God gives for his own amusement. Let us contribute to the purpose of the great stage-manager by making it as vivid and as varied as possible." Surely this saying implies a full appreciation of all the latitudes which the determination to regard life as an art permits, and the injunction with which it concludes conceals under the mildness of irony a moral nihilism which obliterates every possible distinction between the "best" and the "worst" man that history has ever known. Yet Renan himself, like Henry James, was a mild man. Thanks to his early training he retained to the end a sort of sentimental piety and he was compelled to confess that his own life had been more blamelessly studious than he would advise his disciples to make theirs. He did not live by the philosophy which he professed—indeed it is doubtful if any man *could* live by it—and it is to one of his countrymen that one must turn if one would find a still more consistent example of the theory that life is an art.

Anatole France not only professed to regard life from an exclusively aesthetic point of view but came nearer than most of those who would believe that they believe with him to living it according to the principles which he proclaimed. In his works one may find a somewhat softened and idealized picture of his character and opinions and in the two memoirs composed by his maliciously observant secretary, Mr. Henri Brousson, one may find revealed aspects of both which France himself would hardly have cared to see set down. Brousson had a genius for remembering the most telltale gestures as well as the most self-revelatory remarks and he records one utterance of his master which says more in fewer words than even Renan was able to say in his two accomplished sentences.

It seems that the conversation had turned (as in France's company it nearly always did) to the subject of the cult of Venus Pandemos. Some anecdotes were told concerning the practices of those whose tastes ran in the direction usually called "against nature," and some remarks were made concerning both the horror with which many regarded such practices and the ferocity with which the law of many lands punishes those who have been found guilty of them. But France, as usual, professed a very tolerant attitude.

One must gratify whatever tastes one has and seek whatever happiness one may be able to find. *Chacun,* he concluded with a shrug of his shoulders, *fait son salut comme il peut.*

Chacun fait son salut comme il peut. No phrase of English translation can be quite so neat. "Every one seeks his salvation as he may" is awkward, but it expresses in clumsy fashion the idea, and when taken in connection with the context it will give some idea both of the comprehensive liberty there granted and of that sweeping refusal to make moral distinctions which is implied in the masterfully malicious adroitness with which the single word *salut* is made to include any desire which a man may have, from Augustine's thirst for God on down to the last perverse whim which has taken possession of the debauchee whose desires are, no doubt, just as imperious and as little to be questioned as are those of any one else.

Nothing could illustrate a more complete achievement of that inclusive tolerance which has been one of the principal ends proposed to itself by the modern spirit and nothing, perhaps, could be more reasonable. "There are," said Havelock Ellis in a very penetrating phrase, "no hard facts except the facts of emotion." We feel what we feel and we want what we want with a directness which permits of no possible skepticism. We may doubt the conclusions of our logic, the premises of our philosophy, and even the evidence of our eyes, but we cannot doubt these emotions and these desires, since they are for us the only ultimate realities in the sense that they are the only things with which we are in immediate contact. And if this be true what folly it is either to refuse to be guided by the only things of which we have any real knowledge or to pretend to reprobate others who do the same. Life is not a science but rather an art to be lived by each person in accordance with the rules of his own being. Nature has no ends consonant with or comprehensible to the desires of man which would make it possible for him to accord himself to her, and there is nothing outside of Nature except man himself. To one placed far enough away in space and time, to the One whom we may imagine to be so placed, the universe is a thrilling spectacle. Let us do what we can to make it as vivid and as varied as possible. *Chacun fait son salut comme il peut.*

And yet, logical as that may seem, it will not work. The individual man may profess to believe that he finds such a creed satisfactory and he may possibly live out a life by it, but no society organized upon such principles could possibly last. Nature would not tolerate a humanism so complete and would wipe out the animals who dared try to exist upon principles so completely antithetical to those necessary for animal survival. Perhaps man cannot believe anything except that, but he cannot believe it and live, although almost any false science of life will serve to give that regularity necessary to the maintenance of human society. Moral codes which were not only utterly unreasonable but which included among their details prescriptions in themselves as inimical to survival as periodic human sacrifices on a large scale have given a stability which served to perpetuate human society, but aesthetic principles will not do because, though the human mind may be made to work in accordance with them, external nature will not, and the ultimate dilemma may be stated thus: The proposition that life is a science is intellectually indefensible; the proposition that life is an art is pragmatically impossible.

IV

In the world which he describes the artist is God. Not only does he create the characters who move across his pages and control the various destinies accorded them, but he establishes as well the psychological laws according to which the souls of his creatures operate and he makes over even Nature herself when it is necessary to do so in order that his mimic world may seem what he wants it to be. According to the style which he has adopted he may or he may not take care to make it seem that the universe with which he as an artist is concerned appears identical or nearly identical with that in which his readers live, but whether he seeks to produce an illusion of actuality or whether he leaves it clearly apparent that he is describing things, not as they are, but merely as they might be, the fact remains that he is master of the scene to an extent impossible outside of art.

It has often been pointed out that the novel with a thesis is, in spite of the great popularity which the genre has achieved, completely worthless so far as its avowed purpose is concerned since a thesis cannot be proved by means of examples which its defender is at liberty to invent, but deductions far more important than this may be drawn from the omnipotence of the artist so far as his work of art is concerned and it is indeed just the fact that this omnipotence, necessary to the artist, is possible for him *as an artist* but impossible for him *as a man* which reduces the statement that life is an art to mere nonsense when the attempt is made to consider it as more than a pretty phrase. The artist creates the world in which his imagination functions, but the world in which he lives is created for him and he cannot make life the material of an art because he lacks that complete control over both outward events and their inward reverberations which would be necessary to enable him to do so. Many of the most beautiful and satisfactory universes imagined in art bear very little relation to any part of the actual universe even though the characters who move through them have historical names, and it would be easy to show how impossible the artistic success which they achieve in their imaginary world would have been in the real one.

Consider for example the universe of Racine, characterized through its whole extent by a certain orderly sort of grandeur which just barely escapes the pomposity of the French court and which accords so well with the neat couplets in which he chronicled both the deeds of the mortals who inhabited it and the reflections of the punctilious gods who judged them according to the principles laid down in some celestial Book of Etiquette. Racine's characters devote their lives to the pursuit of one fiction called Glory and they are guided or restrained by another fiction called Honor. Neither of these fictions corresponds either to anything in the natural universe or, at least very exactly, to any imaginary thing which ever controlled the lives of any real people. Glory is something won in vague wars between the monarchs of shadowy kingdoms in the course of which none of those inglorious slaughters and devastations which accompany all real wars take place; and Honor is some rhetorical something which has nothing whatever to do with that Christian conception with which it is, nevertheless, in many of the plays equated nor with that complex of conventions mingled with desires for safety and power which are sometimes given that name by people who read enough literature to wish to impose upon themselves a form belonging properly to art.

And yet in that universe in which the action of Racine's tragedies takes place these fictions are real because he has the power to hypothesize for them the same sort of reality which feelings have for real men. He has created the laws of a psychology by virtue of which his characters act in a certain way. He has been able to annihilate facts which, like the horrors of war, might dim the Glory of those heroes of his who so wantonly embark upon it; and he has even been able to make his powers extend to the gods themselves, who judge as he wants them to judge and interpose to set things right when he wishes them to do so. Thanks to these powers his world is neat and satisfactory and simple and his characters live good lives more successfully than any lived in this more complicated world of nature.

To achieve all this, to create a world in which we enter gladly and which we find indeed preferable in many respects to the one in which we live, Racine needed only to be self-consistent, to make his characters act always in accord with the laws of *his* psychology no matter how much they might violate those of real human character and to make things turn out as they would in *his* universe no matter how different this might be from the way in which they would turn out in the world of nature. But the man who, enamored of Racine's world and convinced that life is an art, should determine to live like one of these characters would soon discover that he lacked the necessary power to transform our universe into that of Racine. His wars would not be bloodless, the other characters would not play up to his rôle as they should, and the gods would not intervene when necessary to redress those balances which nature is never very careful to keep even. Indeed we may add that it was exactly this that the king who ruled in Racine's age, together with the various heroes, knights, and lovely ladies who composed his court, did try to do, or rather, of course, if we wish to be more literal, that Racine's world was the world toward which this court was striving and that the difference between the greatness of Racine's tragedies and the littleness of French history is exactly the measure of the difference between the success that can be achieved in art and the failure which is inevitable in life. Bajazet is a satisfactory tragic hero; Louis XIV is not.

We classify works of art into different genres, calling them tragedies or comedies or farces according to the kind of self-contained perfection which they achieve, and in art, though in art alone, it is possible to achieve the requisite purity of style. Tragedy takes place in an imaginary world where everything—language and manners as well as events and emotions—is consonant with that idea of human dignity upon which Tragedy depends. Comedy takes place in an entirely different world where the mind is always superior to the emotions and where, in a word, what we call the Comic Spirit holds exactly the same *exclusive* sway as the Tragic Spirit holds in Tragedy; while Farce takes place in still a third world, and each of the other genres has, in similar fashion, its own realm. One touch of Comedy would destroy any tragedy (unless, of course, as is the case with Shakespeare, the comic scenes were kept insulated from instead of integrated with the others), and one touch of Tragedy would destroy any comedy because that inward harmony, that perfect accord of one part with another, which makes possible the satisfying perfection of a work of art is dependent upon the fact that the whole is organized upon one logical and consistent scheme. But these separate, self-contained, and self-justifying worlds exist only in the imagination of man who created them out of his own desire for harmony rather than as the result of any observation of the real world which is not a tragic nor a comic but rather a natural world—one, that is to say, in which events take place in accordance with laws which have no relation to that human sense of fitness so agreeably exemplified in the worlds of his imagination.

Thus what in art we call Tragedy and Comedy and Farce do not represent life as it was ever lived by any group of people but only the various forms toward which various people or various societies have endeavored unsuccessfully to aspire. Louis XIV tried to live as though he were the hero of one of Racine's trage-

dies; Sir Philip Sydney tried to live as though he were
the hero of one of those half-pastoral, half-heroic prose
romances of which he gave the world an example;
Byron as though he were his own Childe Harold; and
all the members of the society of King Charles II's day
as though they were characters in one of Congreve's
comedies. In each case one may easily divine what style
these various people were seeking to achieve, just as
one has no difficulty in recognizing the fact that the
American self-made man tries to act as though life
were an Alger book or the average Italian as though it
were an opera; but in no single one of the cases could
the rôle be sustained or the catastrophe be made suitable to the work of art upon which the life was modeled. Tragedy may exist in the pages of Racine and
Comedy may exist in the pages of Congreve, but
neither can exist except upon premises invented by
the author for the purpose of constructing a world far
more regular and simple than the real one.

Turn first to a comedy like *Love for Love* or *The
Way of the World* and turn them to some history or
memoir dealing with the actual society out of which
these two works of art were born. There can, to begin
with, be no question concerning the fact that the principal assumptions upon which Congreve proceeded in
the writing of his plays are exactly the same as those
upon which his contemporaries endeavored to proceed in the living of their lives. To the one as to the
other the pursuit of love was the chief business of existence, and love, as the grave Bishop Burnet said in attempting to describe the particular nature of King
Charles's gallant proclivities, "had no seraphic part."
Life was a game, the idea of morality, sexual or other,
was abolished, and the Ten Commandments of which
Charles was said to take no account were discarded in
favor of the ten thousand which he was said never to
break. Wit, address, and *savoir-faire* came to be the
qualities by which the success of a man was judged

and the meaning of any event was sought in the examples of these qualities which were revealed in the course of it, just as the meaning of an event would, by a Puritan, be sought in the moral principles to be deduced therefrom or, by a sentimentalist, in the various tender feelings to which it gave rise.

Proceeding on these assumptions, Congreve wrote what are perhaps the most perfect comedies which universal literature affords. Not only do they glitter with wit but, and this is the thing which makes them supremely great, they present the image of a world which is balanced, harmonious, and perfect. His heroes achieve completely the style which they are seeking to achieve, they play the rôles which they have chosen with flawless skill, and they conduct the action to a conclusion perfectly in accord with that scheme of justice which is not, to be sure, the scheme of justice imagined by Shakespeare any more than it is that imagined by St. Augustine but which is, nevertheless, quite as consistent as either. Every character gets the reward or the punishment due to his wit and address or to his lack of both, and each, that is to say, lives in a universe which functions perfectly according to those ideas of what is right and proper naturally deducible from the premises of Comedy.

If they be considered purely as works of art, it would be folly to say that these comedies are any less admirable than the tragedies of Shakespeare, since they achieve their purpose quite as completely; and if life is an art there is no reason why men may not just as reasonably decide to live according to the model of Congreve as according to the model of Shakespeare. And yet, if one turns now to the histories or the memoirs which deal with the careers of those who did attempt so to live, one will not find there any corresponding perfection. None of Congreve's characters are dead, like Lord Rochester, at thirty, and none dies, like Villiers, "in the worst inn's worst room." Tragedy, melodrama, and that merely frowzy sort of actuality which cannot be likened to any art form, do not intrude upon his scene to spoil it completely as they did upon the scene where Charles's courtiers were doing their best to play their comic rôles as artistically as possible.

Nor can it be said that the fault lay with these comedians. The Rochesters and the Sedleys and the Grammonts were endowed with a wit and an impudence hardly inferior to that of a Valentine or a Mirabell, and if they failed they did so because there was no *milieu* where they could play their rôles with real success. Congreve had created his world out of various fictions, and it was only in such a world that such characters could really live. Since wit was their sole attribute he had imagined a world where wit alone would count, and he had abstracted from it whatever was capable of disturbing the particular sort of harmony which wit can create. Since they were to play with love as one plays a game, without seeking either sensual pleasure or exalted emotions, he gave to them neither hearts which could suffer nor bodies which could be soiled; and thanks to their freedom from the possibility of either emotional complications or physical ills they could flutter like immortal butterflies from intrigue to intrigue—pure intelligences forever fresh, and forever gay. But it is only in art and never in life that the world can be thus reconstructed. Nature gave to the Rochesters and the Sedleys corruptible bodies and even, in certain measure, suffering hearts, without asking whether or not they would like to have them, and thus they lacked that omnipotence which alone would make it possible to consider life as an art.

v

Every good statue is marked by a certain air of repose; every fine picture exists in a state of stable equilibrium brought about by the balance of its masses; and every great work of literature conveys to the reader a certain sense that a peace of some sort reigns within the domain which it describes. No matter how tumultuous some of the events or how far the individual characters with which it is concerned may be from any repose, yet the whole *is* a whole rather than a collection of fragments and does so balance tumult against tumult as to create an order out of disorder and give to the reader that sense of repose which enables him to recognize it as a work of art as distinguished from either any merely literal chronical of life or life itself. Some God, it says, is in some Heaven, even if He be only that creative and omnipotent imagination of the author which has brought order out of chaos and given meaning to the meaningless.

Hence it is that we speak of the Peace of Art and that we take refuge in it from the disorder of nature and of life. We turn to it because, even though it be tragic, it does nevertheless provide balm for the sufferings which it describes and images a world made after a pattern we can understand and accept. And no wonder then that we should like to believe that life itself could be made an art, that we might give to our own existences that roundness achieved by a character in a drama, or that we might somehow impose upon the events taking place around us an order like that assumed by the events which compose any work of art, be it Tragedy or Comedy or Farce. But if it is indeed this kind of peace which we seek, then it is evident that to proceed upon principles deduced from the false analogy between life and art is to court a failure more calamitous even than that of the average man, since those who lived in that fashion—the Louises, the Byrons, and the Rochesters—are the very ones who failed most conspicuously to achieve that peace which St. Augustine on the other hand found in an entirely different manner when he submitted himself completely to the imaginary will of a nonexistent God.

The peace of art is dependent upon order, but the theory that life is an art leads in practice to anarchy.

Art does, in fine, furnish a means by which life may be contemplated, but not a means by which it may be lived. We may survery the history of the world or the events of our past life as an artist surveys his materials. We may make dramas, tragic or farcical, of our memories, and we may to a certain extent arrange them into patterns—noting a striking contrast here, a telling irony there, and a flame of passion somewhere else—even if we cannot compose the whole into a picture as rounded and as perfect as that which constitutes a real work of art for the simple reason that the most imaginative historian can never quite equal the effects of a great novelist. But art ceases where action begins, and its principles cannot afford us that guide to conduct which is the thing which we, our wills paralyzed by our intellects, most need.

Already we have gone further in the direction in which it would lead us than we can safely go. Mind, which has flourished more and more vigorously as animal vitality declined, has reasoned away one by one all those fixed points with reference to which life could be organized and, having first obliterated the faiths to which man could appeal, has turned triumphantly to ask him for what purpose he can live in the world of bare nature or why he should want to do so. And at bottom aesthetics has no answer to these questions, though it may, on the contrary, serve to further that process as the result of which any answer becomes more and more nearly impossible, since it is in reality far more a negation than an affirmation. One can understand very easily the things which it denies—that, for example, life has any inherent purpose or that moral laws, imposed upon man from without, exist—but such denials have already been too effectively made by science and anthropology and logic to require any further reiteration or support. And if one turns to ask what affirmations it brings by way of compensation one discovers that they are either so vague as to be useless or based upon analogies so obviously false that they collapse when submitted to logical examination. At the very best it affords no more than another solvent, another critical instrument by means of which the various sciences of life men used to live by may be proved to be false. If we embrace it we may discover a new way of meditating and perhaps even a new way of despairing, but we know no better than we knew before what we ought to do.

SEVEN

The Phantom of Certitude

T HE man in the street speaks vaguely of "the olden times," for he has but one epithet to apply to all the ages which lie between the dawn of history and the invention of the locomotive. If he thinks of them at all, Julius Caesar and Queen Elizabeth are to him essentially contemporaries, and from his point of view he is quite justified in thinking of them as such since to one who judges of the value of life by the comforts amidst which it is passed it is hardly worth while to make any distinction except that between a way of life which comes up to the nineteenth-century standard and one which does not. All ages except the present were alike in being compelled to get along without the things of which he is most proud, and what he calls "progress" did not begin until a very short time ago.

The telephone, the telegraph, and the cinema—these are things so extraordinarily ingenious that the average man (who does not understand them very well himself) can forgive his remoter ancestors for not having discovered them, but he cannot conceive how they could have consented to get along without some of the simpler comforts, and he concludes that they must have been very poor creatures indeed to have been willing to do so. He shudders to think that they had no bathrooms and if he happens to know anything of social history he is amazed to discover how new what he calls an "old-fashioned lamp" or an "old-fashioned heating stove" really are. He was aware that Aristotle had no electric light but he had never quite imagined him using a smoky wick dipped in a pot of oil scarcely different from that employed by a naked savage in a cave and he is struck by the fact that what he would call the art of living did not even begin until yesterday.

Whole centuries passed, whole civilizations (so called) rose and fell, without the introduction of a single important modification in lighting or heating or transportation. Indeed, real though elementary improvements like the Franklin stove or the oil lamp provided with a chimney to make the flame burn brightly, came so late that they barely had time to become established before they were replaced by still more satisfactory contrivances. Hence, though our average man has been told that Socrates and Plato and even (in their misguided way) Augustine and Aquinas had remarkable brains, he finds it hard to believe. He admits that the inventor of the radio, for instance, had the advantage of accumulated knowledge, but Socrates was in just as good a position as Benjamin Franklin to invent the stove which goes by the latter's name. No recondite knowledge was acquired. Why didn't he do so or why didn't he, at least, confer upon the Greeks some similar blessing instead of leaving them, as he certainly did, quite as uncomfortable as he found them?

Nor is the average man's question quite so foolish as we sometimes pretend it to be. That extraordinary acceleration of the process of invention, that extraordinary speeding up of the process by which man has made himself more and more at home in the physical world and which began, let us say, in the seventeenth century, is not to be accounted for merely by the fact that the knowledge which made it possible had been slowly accumulating. It was, on the contrary, the result of a new orientation of the human mind, of a rather sudden diversion of mental energy into a new channel. Socrates and Plato and Augustine and Aquinas did not invent stoves or improve lamps because it never occurred to them that it was particularly worth while to do so. They held certain views concerning human possibilities and these views implied certain problems whose solution was of primary importance. It was unthinkable that any mind of the first order should concern itself with mere mechanical ingenuity and it did not become thinkable until certain high views concerning human dignity and importance had been reluctantly abandoned.

Francis Bacon made a series of pronouncements concerning the field or scope of future thought. We take his two great works—the *Novum Organum* and *The New Atlantis*—as convenient monuments by which the beginning of the new age may be marked and it is conventional to think of them as constituting a sort of charter of liberty, armed with which man set out to conquer nature. But it is equally possible to regard them in another light and to see them, not as the beginning of one hope but as the final renunciation of another, since their denials are no less sweeping than their affirmations. Bacon claimed all nature as the province of his species, but he renounced at the same time everything which is not included within that apparently comprehensive realm, and in so doing he confined the human spirit within limits so narrow that Socrates or Plato or Augustine or Aquinas would have found them suffocating. Looking back upon centuries of thought and aspiration, he pronounced them just as futile as our Average Man of today would pronounce them, and with a wave of the hand he swept away all the attempts which had ever been made to establish a connection between the human spirit and things which lie above and beyond the world of nature. Forbidding man to seek God, he gave him in exchange full permission to invent as many lamps and stoves as his ingenuity could devise.

Mankind had already discovered for itself the truths on which he insisted and it needed only to have them formulated in order to start eagerly along the road which he indicated. Nor can it be denied that history has afforded him the most irrefutable or pragmatic justifications. What "progress" did the philosophers ever make or what tangible fruits did they ever produce as the result of their labors? Did knowledge of God ever march with the steady stride of science or did theologians ever have the habit of conferring upon mankind recurrent blessings like steam power and surgery? Obviously not. It was only when the thinker discovered how small are the things he can do that he succeeded in doing anything at all, only when he renounced the effort to find the key to heaven that he was able to keep chimneys from smoking, and only after he had stopped believing in the possibility of eternal life that he learned how the gout might be prevented.

Undoubtedly, then, the world has grown steadily more comfortable and the spread of comfort has not been confided to merely physical things. Not only has the rigor of the seasons been modified but the terror of the unknown world has been abolished as well, since he who gives up his hope of heaven may relieve himself at the same time from his fears of hell. The heroic age of the spirit was, like the heroic age of the flesh, a troublesome time. Its heroes were doughty men to whom diabolic visitors were no more unusual than angelic ones and they were as far from that certain humble security which a modern man has a right to feel as they were from the comforts of a suburban villa whose gilded and clanking radiators banish the cold of winter far more effectually than the most picturesque fire roaring up the defective chimney of the most flourishing abbey of the Middle Age. Doubtless there were times when the saint who had lost his ecstasy and was staring into the bottomless pit would have been glad to know that he had no soul to lose and doubtless there were times when the sinner who found repentance hard would have been only too willing to surrender his position at the center of the universe if he could have found a corner in which to hide as remote as we know this little earth of ours to be. We have settled into a sort of bourgeois security, and bourgeois security has its own dull comforts, for if we have not much to gain neither have we much to lose.

But those more ambitious spirits who find it impossible to content themselves with such a vegetative existence and who hope to dramatize it by means of their imagination are wrong if they suppose that they can ever succeed in making life one tenth so luminous as it was to those who felt themselves playing an important part in a cosmic struggle. Renan's advice notwithstanding, we cannot make the spectacle either very vivid or very varied without the co-operation of that universe in which we are only an accident, and the most violent gyrations of the most determined aesthete gesticulating in the void are merely absurd. A Swinburne, disgusted with the tame domesticities of a Tennyson, may re-invent Sin in order to be able to commit it, and a D'Annunzio, furiously impotent, may bellow about Love in order to be able to suffer from it, but all the capital letters in the composing-room cannot make the words more than that which they have become— shadows, as essentially unreal as some of the theological dogmas which have been completely forgotten.

Nor was it until very recent years that any very serious efforts were made to re-expand the world which Bacon had so effectively contracted. In nineteenth-century England, Carlyle and Ruskin constituted themselves prophets of woe crying out in a materialistic wilderness, but neither they nor gentler mystics like Emerson could be called a part of the main stream of thought which flowed swiftly and happily through Baconian channels. Mankind was busy taking possession of that province of nature which had been given it, and its moments of reflection were spent in congratulating itself on the manifold blessings of the new dispensation. The complacency of Macaulay calling on all good bourgeois to examine the past in order that they might appreciate their own good fortune, and the optimism of Huxley beckoning the scientist on to new triumphs—these illustrate most typically the attitude of an age which had not yet either realized all that it was losing or taken the time to consider the meaning of the losses of which it was aware.

Indeed the process by which man was reduced to his present insignificance was carried on with actual joy. Men hailed a new indication that the soul was mortal almost as eagerly as they hailed the invention of a new machine, and the fact that it had now become possible to state with almost positive assurance that we were, in the future, to get the most reliable information concerning the nature of our being by studying in the zoo was proclaimed by Huxley as though it were literally a gospel—a piece, that is to say, of very good news. In part because these various discoveries were vaguely felt to justify that exclusive concern with nature which was resulting in an increasing control over it in the interests of comfort, and in part because men felt, as yet, only the greater security of the natural world, they considered every new indication of their finiteness as a new triumph. Thus all the bases upon which modern despair rests were laid joyously by people who were quite sure that they were serving humanity, and all the chains by which we are now bound so much more firmly to earth than we want to be were forged amidst shouts of triumph.

It would be difficult to say just when the advance of materialism began to lose that air of being a victorious march which certainly characterized its early stages, but there can be no doubt of the fact that today it often hesitates to take possession of regions which, not many years ago, it would have claimed hastily as its own. Even the proponents of Freudianism, certainly the most far-reaching of any of the recent attempts to rob man of such shreds of dignity as had been left to him, sometimes advance their theories with a certain amount of apology and seem anxious to spare whatever the theory makes it possible to spare instead of rushing in, as many of the early materialists did, to take away even more than they had a right to take. And certainly no one who has taken the trouble to familiarize himself with the most recent scientific and philosophical writing can have failed to observe that, whatever its results, it seems animated more and more by a desire to escape from those ultimately materialistic conclusions which slightly earlier philosophical and scientific writers were striving to achieve. If the end of the nineteenth century found thinkers doing their best to confine man within the framework of a mechanistically conceived nature, the first quarter of the twentieth found them eagerly seeking some way, either scientific or metaphysical, by which he may escape from it. Seeds of discontent are spreading in that vast spiritual bourgeoisie which the nineteenth century created, and its ranks are breaking. Who reads Haeckel now or who, having read him, fails to find the complacency of his atheism even more antiquated than his facts?

Indeed nothing is more characteristic of strictly contemporary thought than the multiplication of terms and theories concerning which the clearest thing is the fact that they were born of a desire to avoid the conclusions which, superficially at least, seem most easily to follow from modern knowledge. Perhaps William James with his "will to believe" and Henri Bergson with his "intuition" were the forerunners of these later developments since both were busy with the attempt to establish at least the *possibility* that some loophole might exist through which the soul could escape, and certainly Vaihinger, with his philosophy of the *als ob* and his defense of workable "fictions," struck out upon lines of thought which have for the present generation an immediate appeal which they lacked for his own. But it is during still more recent years that these tentative and often very intangible apologies for a modified and not quite thoroughgoing materialism have multiplied so rapidly as to make it extremely difficult to keep up with them. Even psychology—that "science of the soul" which, paradoxically enough, did not begin to develop until the soul had disappeared—now attempts to retract the conclusions deduced from some of its own demonstrations. Out of England comes the mysterious word "emergence," out of Germany the still more mysterious word *Gestalt,* and though the latter means only "pattern," whole books have been written to prove that it renders materialism *passé.*

Nor have the exponents of the purely physical sciences failed to respond to the influence of this unexpressed desire to escape from a mechanistic universe which is determining the direction of thought in exactly the same insidious way as the opposite desire influenced the scientific and philosophical thought of the late nineteenth century. No hypothesis of the new physics has been so much discussed as the quantum theory, and the popular attention which it has attracted has been, in a very large measure, due to the fact that, abstruse as it is and incomplete as are the data upon which it is based, it is one of those very few scientific hypotheses which may be taken to weaken rather than to reaffirm purely mechanistic interpretations of nature. The layman—even though he have a fair mathematical equipment—is doubtless incapable of understanding it completely, but he can easily perceive, first, that it is based upon the observation of an imperfectly understood anomaly in the behavior of certain of those very minute particles which are supposed to constitute matter and, second, that no one would dare to draw the far-reaching conclusions which are sometimes drawn from it were it not for the fact that they and their readers are very anxious for an excuse to do so.

In our grandfathers' day popular science was rather prone to run ahead of its knowledge in its eagerness to banish God from the universe; in our own it reveals the opposite tendency to let Him (or some attenuated equivalent like the theory of the "organic" character of inanimate nature) in through a back door which may not even be open. Bertrand Russell likes to tell his audience that though we may be compelled to believe that there is no distinction between matter and spirit, yet he is willing to assure them that matter is not so material as we used to think it, and Bertrand Russell can by no means be thought of as furnishing an extreme example of the lengths to which certain contemporary scientific writers are willing to go in the effort to provide some comfort, however attenuated, to their flocks. One popular exponent of the *Gestalt* psychology first promised his readers a satisfactory substitute for the consolation of religion and then ended up with the injunction that, whenever life seemed meaningless or not worth the living, they should remember their obligation "to configurate with the Universe," thus calling to their aid a phrase which, he assured them, was so magically meaningful that it was capable of drawing back the most desperate from the brink of suicide.

The researches of science revealed the emptiness of the universe and the all-pervading "naturalness" of Nature, not resting content until she had swept the furthermost reaches of the sky and demonstrated to everybody's satisfaction that even the remotest nebulae which the spectroscope can reach are composed of the same elements and obey the same laws as those found in our own humble sphere, and yet even science, a little aghast at her own revelations, begins to seem to wish that she could find some way of undoing the work which she did too well. But the humanistic need for the things which science banished outrun her willingness or her capacity to bring them back, and that rebirth of interest in metaphysics to which we must presently turn furnishes a phenomenon even more striking than that afforded by the efforts of the scientist to temper the rigor of his conclusions in the interest of this human need.

Metaphysical thought occupies a proud realm of her own which she rules by her own right. For a good thousand years she did not deign to glance at the facts which the scientist, grubbing the earth or consorting with the animals, had collected in a spirit too humble to allow him to force them upon her attention. During that thousand years she reached many conclusions about the world which she believed to exist over and above the world of nature without bothering to ascertain what Nature herself had to say. Not a few of these conclusions were quite satisfactory within her realm and though, as science grew more powerful, she retired more and more until at last she came to exist only upon tolerance in some vague No Man's Land lying between science on the one hand and mere nonsense on the other, yet she has recently begun to assert herself once more and has raised up defenders to reassert her right to an existence once more entirely independent of her old adversary. Even Neo-Thomism, which began as a purely Roman Catholic philosophy, has attracted students who embrace it upon purely metaphysical grounds, which, they contend, are quite sufficient to make it tenable without calling upon faith for any aid, and a whole group of thinkers are busy building systems which rest upon a renewed assertion that metaphysics can not only demonstrate her right to disregard science entirely but can also, once that right has been granted, furnish the human spirit those reasons for living which science seems to have denied.

The claims of metaphysics are those which we must now consider, but before doing so it was necessary, for the purpose of this essay, to establish the fact that if they have been recently reasserted it is only as the result of a certain desperation. The centuries which have passed since Bacon somewhat cavalierly denied them have seemed only to justify him more and more in his attitude. Thought has come increasingly to depend on the data furnished by science for its material, and it is far more difficult now than it was during the Middle Ages to defend the autonomy of metaphysics. If efforts are made to do so the fact furnishes a striking proof both of the impasse to which the scientific spirit has conducted us and the lengths to which we are willing to go in our efforts to escape from it. Obviously, the "will to believe" is, in many quarters, not lacking today, and if the faiths which result are usually rather vague and unsatisfactory it can only be because our increased knowledge has left it but little scope for its operations.

II

The older metaphysicians of whom Thomas Aquinas may be taken as the most magnificent type seldom felt the need of defending their systems against any knowledge which the mere experimenter revealed. The little that was known of nature could easily be reconciled with the conclusions deduced *a priori,* and Aquinas, by means of the process which Bacon contemptuously likened to that of a spider spinning cobwebs, could draw out of himself materials from which to construct both a comprehensive cosmography and a detailed code of conduct without needing to fear that the gossamer threads by which the weightiest conclusions were sometimes supported would be broken by any rude blows from a natural fact wielded by the hands of an irreverent investigator. It was not until some time later that the Galileos began to harass even the most reckless of those who based their astronomy and their physics on sound theological principles, and there was no pressing need for metaphysics to assert her autonomy, for the simple reason that all the elementary science then existing could be easily digested.

But natural knowledge having grown mightily while metaphysics was forced more and more into a defensive position, the rôles were reversed. The latter was compelled to surrender one field after another to her opponent, withdrawing—reluctantly, perhaps, but nevertheless completely—from the provinces which astronomy, chemistry, geology, medicine, and finally psychology came to occupy, and thus gradually restricting herself until she was on the point of vanishing completely into thin air. She could no longer make any pretense of absorbing science, because science had absorbed her, and when the time at last arrived for a new generation, stifling in the restricted world of nature, to turn to her for deliverance, it was discovered that she had abandoned all the pretensions which would have enabled her to furnish it. Only that philosophy which accepted the conclusions of natural science as its premise was considered intellectually respectable, and such philosophy was too completely the slave of science to furnish any weapon with which the latter could be combated. The only possibility which remained was, therefore, the possibility of turning back to the great metaphysical systems of the pre-Renaissance and of developing the idea—perhaps latent in them—that metaphysics has a right to conclusions independent of and even contrary to the conclusions of science.

Hence it is that all contemporary attempts to dispense with the laboratory and to draw from the mind alone conclusions more satisfactory than those which the laboratory affords must begin with a declaration of independence more specific than was necessary in the days when the latter could hardly be said to exist.

It must begin, that is to say, with the assumption that the universe which the human spirit inhabits is not only not identical with, but also not wholly conditioned by, the world of outside nature, and it must assert the power of the mind itself to discover unaided the verities which exist in the realm where it alone has its being. For a century or two it has been customary to make fun of the desperate expedient adopted by certain early naturalists who, living in terror of the Inquisition, were accustomed to preface their boldest utterances with the warning that what they were about to say was true "philosophically but not theologically." But comic as this sophistry has generally been considered, it is not wholly dissimilar to the defense now sometimes put up by metaphysicians, long accustomed to bow to the decrees of science as the earlier scientist bowed to the decrees of the church, who argue in favor of the possibility that certain "human" truths may exist quite independent of the scientific truths which cannot contradict them because the two occupy completely separate realms.

Such a conception cannot be held by anyone who is not willing to reject the fundamental tendency which unifies all thought since the Renaissance, and it is greatly to the credit of the young Cambridge student T. E. Hulme, whose *Speculations* have been widely admired by the new metaphysicians, that he recognized this fact and began his book with this sweeping statement: "One of the main achievements of the nineteenth century was the elaboration and universal application of the principle of *continuity*. The destruction of this conception is, on the contrary, an urgent necessity of the present."

Perhaps all the implications of this dogmatic statement are not immediately apparent, but they will become so when it is recalled that the tyranny which scientific thought has come to exercise over the human spirit became possible as the result of a process in the course of which the various phenomena of which the consciousness is aware were made part of one great whole. When, for example, Darwin proclaimed his theory of the descent of man he forged a link between zoology and ethics, two departments of study which an early naturalist—Pliny, let us say—would have considered entirely independent of one another; and though the result of Darwin's establishment of a continuity by means of which one might carry conclusions over from the one to the other was fraught with particularly evident consequences, this link of his was only one of the many by means of which the now generally admitted continuity of all the sciences was established. Thus, for example, the comparatively recent investigations into the atomic and sub-atomic structure of matter have made meaningless the once fundamental distinction between physics and chemistry, while, to take a still more striking case, psychology has attempted, not only to bridge the gulf between the physiology of the brain and the processes of thought, but also to make aesthetics a part of that psychology which is itself a part of physiology. The categories into which human knowledge was once divided have thus seemed to cease to represent any real distinction and to have become purely artificial divisions of that one and only subject which is called natural science.

It is over the bridges thus established that scientific materialism has passed, taking possession of each field of human speculation as soon as a connection had been established between that field and the realm which had already been acknowledged as her own. Speaking roughly we may say that before the beginning of the eighteenth century physical investigation had completely displaced both deductive logic and the appeal to authority so far as physics, chemistry, and astronomy were concerned and that metaphysical thought had completely abandoned any claim which she might have upon them, while feeling perfectly secure in her right to rule all the other departments of human knowledge such as, for instance, aesthetics, ethics, and religion. But before the end of that century the natural science called biology had taken possession of the whole realm of living matter and thus proclaimed her right to that vast and heretofore apparently untraversable region which, if a political metaphor may be permitted, seemed to lie like a buffer state between that dead material which belonged to the scientist and that world of thoughts and feelings which seemed completely different from it. To the earlier thinker the important thing about living matter was that it *lived;* to the scientist the important thing about it was that it was *matter,* and there is all the difference in the world between the two emphases. Thanks to the latter, the nineteenth century saw the methods of scientific investigation carried into every department of human activity and the data of physical science used as the basis on which every effort to understand either the natural or the human worlds was founded, while the beginning of the twentieth saw the last vestige of a distinction between the various kinds of knowledge wiped away in such fully developed materialistic systems as the Watsonian psychology which regards thought as an unimportant physiological phenomenon and physiology itself as only a branch of that branch of physics which, for no reason except tradition, is still called chemistry.

In view of these facts, the fundamental character of Hulme's central dogma becomes clear. If metaphysical thought is to reassert its right to reach its own conclusions in certain fields it can do so only by making them inaccessible to natural science, and it can make them inaccessible only by destroying the connections between one and the other. Since thought has never been observed except in connection with certain physiological processes, science concludes that thought is a physiological phenomenon and since, to

take another example, morality can be shown to have
arisen when a certain sacrosanct authority was attributed to tribal customs, scientific history concludes that
Morality is only another name for Mores.

But metaphysics would deny the validity of both of
these conclusions. It would insist that thought as we
know it is so entirely different from physiology as we
know it, and Morality in its fully developed form so
entirely different from tribal custom, that the attempt
to equate them, to apply deductions made concerning
the nature of the one to the nature of the other, is
wholly unjustified. It would, to put it briefly, deny that
dead matter passes into living matter and living matter into thought by a continuous process or that customs become morals by a similarly *continuous* process.
It would, on the other hand, insist that there exists
between these two an unbridgeable gulf which sepa-
rates one from another, that there is, if you like, an
instant when—or a point at which—one brusquely
ceases to be the other and comes to be wholly itself.

It may, indeed, be added that certain schools of
the most recent scientific thought which, as has already been remarked, show an equally eager desire to
discover some means by which the mind might escape
from the materialistic tyranny have been endeavoring
to formulate scientific conceptions which would permit the existence of these discontinuities which it was
exactly the effort of earlier science to break down.
Thus, for example, the central fact which the quantum
theory attempts to explain is an apparent discontinuity
in the behavior of minute particles of matter and the
very modish psychological theory of emergence is a
theory which proposes to account for such complex
psychological realities as the thing which we call personality by considering it not as the simple aggregate
of instincts or reflexes (conditioned and inherited) but
as consisting of something quite new which comes
into being or, as they say, *emerges* from the pattern

formed by the elements which compose this aggregate, and which is quite distinct from it.

Nor is it difficult to understand the results which might arise from this rupture of the supposed continuity of nature and the re-establishment of ethics and aesthetics as separate and autonomous realms. If they are not part of the natural world, then it is at least possible that they have meanings which it does not have and at least possible that these meanings may be discovered by methods—deductive logic, for example—which had been discarded as instruments for the pursuit of truth simply because they were not fruitful when applied to problems which arise in connection with this merely natural world.

Thus if the rupture which Hulme proclaimed were to be actually effected it might make once more possible the development of various aesthetic and moral "sciences" which need have no more accord with natural science than was necessary in the days before the continuity had been established. It would not, to be sure, do more than establish this possibility and it would certainly not in itself in any way determine the nature or tendency of such possible aesthetic or moral sciences, but it is at least a straw and the opponents of materialism have been reduced to that condition in which straws seem worth grasping at.

III

Now whatever one may think of the direction which scientific thought took during the last few centuries, it cannot be denied that it *had* a direction which could be clearly perceived. When all allowance has been made for differences of opinion, we may still say that scientists agreed in reaching the same conclusions and we may point out an interesting paradox. While theology maintained that it could demonstrate the absolute certitude of its conclusions and proclaimed the necessity for everyone's thinking alike, theologians persisted in disagreeing among themselves. Science, on the other hand, never ceased (in theory at least) to admit the tentative nature of its theories nor to encourage independent experiment, and yet scientists came more and more to agree in accepting the same tentative hypotheses, while theologians disagreed more and more violently concerning the "certitudes" at which each individual had arrived.

In view of this fact we should not be surprised to discover that the new metaphysicians who agree in regarding the supposed continuity between man and nature as in reality nonexistent agree in nothing else and have broken up into various schools. Since the immediate result of denying the competence of science to interfere in the realm of aesthetics, morals, and religion was simply to re-establish a liberty to believe whatever one happens to want to believe, those who considered themselves endowed with such liberty have turned in as many different directions as their individual natures led them to prefer. Thus while certain among them have embarked upon genuine and arduous metaphysical studies, encouraged by a rebirth of the medieval hope that metaphysical certitudes (rather more secure than the "truths" of natural science) could be arrived at by pure thought, others, with no real taste for the metaphysical discipline, have simply thanked it hastily for their deliverance and then gone over to the faiths from which rationalism had formerly kept them, as, for example, G. K. Chesterton went over to the Catholicism which had always been temperamentally attractive to him.

With these Neo-Catholics, Neo-Anglicans, and even (perhaps) Neo-Baptists and Neo-Mormons we need have no particular concern. To the man who not only accepts the statement of a Hulme that the continuity between man and nature has been broken but who takes that statement to mean simply that he may believe whatever he likes, there are possible just

exactly as many new faiths as there were old ones and
he need only attach "Neo" to any one of the names by
which they formerly passed in order to constitute himself a philosopher. The addition of the syllable will
not, however, prevent them from being essentially
anachronistic because they would be unsuited to modern society even if the grip of materialism should be
broken, and they are too clearly mere survivals to be
considered a part of any contemporary movement
of the mind or spirit. But in so far as a revival of the
metaphysical as opposed to the scientific approach to
the problems of existence results in any novel attempts
to solve them, it is a part of the concern of this essay,
which must consider the replies which the proponents
of such an approach would make to the dilemmas
which the essay has endeavored to describe.

Fundamentally, perhaps, the new metaphysics owes
rather more to that pragmatism which was an off-
shoot of the scientific method than its proponents
would always care to admit, and certainly its point
of view may be easily approached via pragmatism itself, which proposed a new test of truth whose relation
to the truths of science may here be briefly recalled.

When the scientist is faced with a certain number
of isolated facts he is accustomed to account for them
by accepting pro tem that hypothesis consistent with
the facts which appears to be most useful for the purpose of the investigation which he is attempting to
carry out, and the two questions which he asks concerning any hypothesis are simply, first, can it be disproved and, second, if not, how useful can it be made?
If the answer to the first of these questions is "no" and
the answer to the second is "more useful than any
other which has been proposed," then the scientist
accepts it as the one upon whose assumptions he will
proceed. Ordinarily, however, the scientist recognizes
a distinction between such an accepted hypothesis and
that Truth which may emerge when more facts are

discovered, while pragmatism proposed to him that such a distinction be abolished.

Consistency with known facts and fruitful workability are, it said, the only characteristics by which we would ever be able to recognize Truth if we found it, and consequently should constitute a definition of Truth itself. If the skeptic says that all so-called truths are merely workable hypotheses, we, said the pragmatist, will affirm on the contrary that all workable hypotheses are truths. Ptolemaic astronomy was "true" as long as it explained all known facts and proved fruitful so far as the regulation of the calendar and all the other uses to which it was put were concerned; it became "untrue" only when facts which it could not explain were discovered and when the Copernican hypothesis proved still more useful for practical developments.

And though this pragmatic point of view no doubt owed its development to the scientific spirit, its applicability in realms which science does not control are immediately apparent. In the hands of William James it became a defense of the rights of a will to believe—not, as seems sometimes to be assumed, whatever you would like to believe but whatever would be useful and *not inconsistent with the known facts*. It would, for instance, hardly permit the most glowing faith to maintain that the sun goes around the earth, because it recognizes the revolution of the earth around the sun as "known fact," but it would, on the other hand, permit or rather encourage it to assume the truth of all cheerful propositions concerning the immortality of the soul, the ultimate though hidden benevolence of nature, etc., which could not be definitely disproved, since, according to this system of thought, anything may legitimately be regarded as true provided only that it is (1) pleasant to believe and (2) not clearly demonstrable as false.

Now James, with his taste for science, lived, it must

be remembered, in a world where there were a good many "known facts," and though he was widely tolerant of even the most fantastically dogmatic religions when they were embraced by others he was compelled to restrict the exercise of his own will to believe within the limits set by the facts which he knew and to rest content with a rather vague confidence that the world was "somehow good" even though such a belief could rest upon nothing stronger than desire plus the fact that its falsity was not demonstrated with absolute finality. But James, it must be further remembered, hardly attempted to deny that *continuity* of which we have been speaking, since he at least appeared tacitly to admit the relevance of physical fact to metaphysical discussion and would probably have been willing to maintain that a chemical analysis of the wine used in the sacrament would be sufficient to disprove the doctrine of transubstantiation in its most literal form. If, however, the continuity between man and nature is assumed to be broken, then the field for the exercise of the will to believe is enormously increased since no "known fact" about nature *can* disprove any proposition which concerns man alone and since, therefore, its truth (all science notwithstanding) may be demonstrated by its usefulness alone (if one is a pure pragmatist) or by its usefulness plus logical demonstration (if one is a metaphysician).

Hence many thinkers who regard this discontinuity as established believe that they can return to the methods of pre-Renaissance thought and re-establish both morals and religion upon a basis which natural science cannot discredit. They will begin, if necessary, with general propositions like Descartes' "I think, therefore I am," and they will proceed by logical means to deduce one proposition after another until they have deduced not only a cosmography more suited to man than that of natural science but also a system of morals by which he can live successfully. Aquinas, whom they much admire, did succeed, they point out, in constructing such a system, and they see no reason why they should not do so also if purely naturalistic criticism is disposed of first.

However fruitful the methods of natural science may have proved themselves when applied to the solution of purely natural problems, they have been, such philosophers would insist, entirely unfruitful when applied to problems of another order, and they have therefore established no right to concern themselves with them. If physics and chemistry and biology have flourished, morals, religion, and aesthetics have withered. Since science destroyed the first, undermined the second, and attempted to reduce the third to a department of psychopathology, the only hope for any one of them rests on its re-establishment as a distinct category of study entirely separate from any other. Let us therefore (say metaphysicians) found a new system of religion, a new science of morals, and a new philosophy of aesthetics, without going outside the realm of each one for the fundamental principles on which it is to be founded. Moral systems are useful, and moral systems may be made perfectly consistent with themselves. Let us forget tribal custom and the comparative study of ethical systems. Let us turn to pure logic and out of it let us construct a serviceable code.

Perhaps most of the new metaphysicians have not got much further than that and have been compelled for the moment to rest content with demonstrating to their own satisfaction, not what morality is, but simply that, science notwithstanding, there may possibly be such a thing. Certainly none of them has yet produced a Summa which, like that of St. Thomas, begins with the most general propositions and ends by codifying the answers to the most specific questions concerning the minutiae of conduct. Perhaps indeed they have been restrained from doing so by the fact that the most ardent modern metaphysician and the warmest admirer of Aquinas's metaphysical subtlety can hardly read his *magnum opus* without smiling at some of his conclusions and without realizing that such a metaphysical structure, proceeding as it does from one proposition to another without checking its deductions by reference to any external facts, is likely to be fantastically awry at the top as the result of an almost imperceptible error somewhere near the bottom. But in any event their ethical systems are, for the most part, rather general and consist chiefly in the statement that if a belief in ethics is favorable both to the health of society and the spiritual development of the individual, then ethics may and should be regarded as a legitimate field of study.

Science, to be sure, cannot prove that any "spirit not ourselves" desires that men be honest; science may even assert from its study of the origin of morality in primitive societies that a belief in good and evil as mystical realities grew up merely as a result of the practical value of such a belief and may add that, such being the case, it cannot see how a scientific mind can sanction the assumption that good and evil are anything more than the names which any given society is accustomed to bestow upon things in or out of accord with its customs. But metaphysics would reply, first, that ethics may have *emerged* from custom at some instance when the two ceased to be in any way continuously related to one another and, second, that this possibility is transformed into a certitude by the fact that a belief in it results in a flowering of the human spirit.

Now this fundamental attitude is capable of appearing under various guises. It may even form the basis for a renewed acceptance of some old religious faith, and the statement that the human world has somehow emerged from the natural world with which it no longer forms a continuum may be given either a very literal or a very abstruse interpretation. It may be taken to mean that two different sorts of reality equally solid and "really real" exist side by side in spite of the fact that they never touch and that, for example, the statement that morality and mores are identical may be completely true in one realm and completely false in the other, or it may, on the other hand, be taken only as a sort of metaphor which is used to suggest that certain fictions like "morality" may be made to serve our purpose quite as well as they would if they had a real existence in nature. Perhaps some might go even so far as to maintain that the distinction here made between a reality and a workable fiction is a meaningless distinction, and certainly this more or less metaphorical way of interpreting the nature of spiritual realities is the more characteristically modern way by virtue of the fact that it is the one most distinctly different from that adopted by the ordinary medieval mind, which saw no distinction whatsoever between a principle of physics and a principle of morality.

Having, then, assumed certain propositions *a priori* and having deduced from them the consequences which follow when they are made the bases of logical deduction, the metaphysical moralist recommends them to us with an argument somewhat as follows. It is admitted that moral and spiritual certitudes are useful both to the individual and to society. Science has failed to furnish either, but logic is capable of supplying both. Take what she has to offer, live by the principles which she proclaims *as though* they were true, and you will discover that they either *are* true or at least, what is really the same thing, that they will work *as though they were*.

Thus the purpose of metaphysics may be considered as, in its own way, a proposal to make life an art, and in certain respects the way which it proposes reveals a truer conception of the essential nature of art than does that of those aesthetes like Renan or Anatole

France who assume that they are making an art of life when they adopt nihilistic principles although, as a matter of fact, art is distinguished from life by the fact that movements within its framework are controlled by laws more numerous and more narrow than those which control the movements of life itself. The metaphysical effort to base life on fiction is, on the other hand, actually analogous to the effort of the artist who merely assumes that certain values exist and that certain moral or psychological principles operate and then proceeds to construct in his imagination a world where they actually do so. The theologian who believed in the fiction called grace and who lived as though he were able to pipe that grace for his own use did unconsciously make life an art in a far truer sense than Anatole France ever succeeded in making it, and it is he rather than the Frances and the Renans that the metaphysician would have us imitate.

Assuming, then, that life is an art, he too bids us live it as such, but instead of interpreting the injunction to mean that we should deny the existence of all eternal values and declare ourselves free from all moral codes, he proclaims the primary importance of the realities or the fictions without which art is impossible. If natural science has not only played havoc in the human world but also so monopolized the word "science" itself that we can no longer speak of a "science of living," then let us, by all means, speak of life as an art, but let us remember that it is an art whose proper style may be logically deduced and that the "fictions" necessary for the achievement of that style are the things which we call metaphysical certitudes.

IV

Since the time when science first began to destroy more than it knew it was destroying and since materialism first began to annex one province after another without realizing that it was soon to possess the entire universe, there has never, perhaps, been any attempt to escape from both materialism and science as determined as that which the metaphysical movement represents and there has never, perhaps, been any which seemed so subtly defensible. If the belief that man and nature are discontinuous realities should ever come to be universally accepted, not merely as a fine-spun theory but as a fact which our minds had absorbed as completely as they have absorbed certain elements of the scientific creed, then the world in which we have our being would undergo another transformation hardly less complete than that which it underwent at the Renaissance.

The door into the unseen world would be open once more and religion might well flourish quite as luxuriantly as it did in former times. Probably all those beliefs which men have always held when permitted to do so—beliefs, that is to say, in immortality, in the existence of an external moral order, and in the omnipresence of a "spirit not ourselves"—would arise again, while Love and Honor and Nobility would once more come to seem living realities. Nor is this all, for Terror would probably be born again along with Hope. We know from experience what metaphysics can do when freed from the necessity of referring her conclusion to the test of external fact, we know how detailed are the certitudes which she can reach, and we may assume that she would once more conclusively demonstrate the existence, not only of a real Heaven, but of a real and flaming Hell as well.

When the rights of science were first asserted no one guessed how fundamentally it would alter our view of the universe, and no one who reasserts the rights of metaphysics can say just how far an acceptance of them would lead us. Were they generally and fully admitted, mankind might find itself a century hence in a world which would seem to us very curiously compounded of medieval and modern elements—in a world, that is to say, which would be externally very much like the present one but internally far more like the world of Augustine or of Calvin. Having come to accept as fundamental the proposition which asserts the absolute discontinuity of man and nature, it might continue to build its machines according to the laws of mechanics while it might regulate its conduct by, and take its faith from, the pages of some new Summa whose specific statements concerning moral conduct and spiritual cosmography would seem to us as fantastically unreconcilable with scientific naturalism as do those of St. Thomas himself.

And if it is difficult to believe in such a future as this, if the mind which admits the ingenuity of the metaphysicians' proposition refuses nevertheless to grant the possibility of the results which would seem to follow upon its acceptance, the fact is due less to any fallacy in the reasoning than to the fact that the metaphysical faith is marked by a certain tenuosity which seems to condemn it to remain academic and which renders it unlikely ever to translate itself into terms capable of affecting the everyday life of society. The continuity which it denies is, as a matter of fact, exactly the thing in which, rightly or wrongly, we most easily believe. It is tacitly accepted by people too little accustomed to abstract thought even to know that they accept it and the "possibility" which its opponents advance makes no reference to ordinary experience in spite of the fact that all living faiths have always been based upon an acceptance rather than upon a denial of "continuity," as the almost universal appeal to the evidence of miracles will show.

Vague and abstruse as any religion erected upon such a metaphysical foundation must of necessity be, it is doubtless the most substantial possible to modern man, but we need only ask what a believer of the past would think of it in order to realize how feeble it is when considered, not as an ingenious mental exercise but as a means of combating either that moral nihilism which is fatal to society or that spiritual despair which falls upon the individual victim of an all-embracing materialistic philosophy. Fictions served to guide and to control many rebellious generations, but they could do so only because they were not known to be fictions, and they lose their power as soon as we recognize them as such. Contemporary theologians, driven as they are to the last extremity, may eagerly hail the feeble sanction of an "as if," but they must realize that it is not very satisfactory even as a *faut de mieux* and that though they may proclaim it as an evidence of faith reborn they must admit that this belief in a re-mote and singularly shadowy region where spiritual values are supreme is a very unsatisfactory substitute for the belief that such values are supreme throughout all the universe.

We may reasonably doubt whether men can actually live by any faith so tenuous and hence we may rea-sonably doubt that it is destined ever to exist outside the pages of a book or to exercise any real influence upon a world in which science has triumphed exactly because its theories, its demonstrations, and its re-sults were so exceedingly substantial. Reacting against that science, many thinkers have realized its various defects and its failure to provide many things of which the human spirit has need, but they have been far less successful in any effort to break its grip. Thanks to this reaction one may today hear youth once more speaking with enthusiasm of "authority" whose destruction by science was hailed by the youth of yes-terday and of those "certitudes" which that same science banished amidst similar demonstrations of joy, but the need for re-establishing them is far more clearly evident than the means by which any such re-establishment may be effected.

This science, once so much loved but now so much

feared, has won an ascendancy over us and holds us whether we will or no. Testing her conclusions wherever they were capable of being tested, demonstrating her power to control the realm in which she rules, she has not only won from us a confidence in her methods but also made it well-nigh impossible for us to believe in any others. Whenever she has joined battle with Pure Thought over any conclusion, the truth or falsity of which could be definitely established, it is she who has carried away the victory, and under the circumstances it is not strange that we should, even in spite of ourselves, have more confidence in her inferences than in those of an enemy so often defeated. We may turn to metaphysics and we may wish that we could repose a supreme confidence in her, but we know that she was demonstrably wrong in so many of the "certitudes" which science has unquestionably upset that we find it hard to build many hopes upon those established by methods so little sure that they were once capable of proving that the sun revolved around the earth quite as conclusively as they can now be said to prove anything else. We may wish that we could believe what she assures us that we may, but a skepticism pointing to the past for its confirmation whispers to us that metaphysics may be, after all, only the art of being sure of something that is not so and logic only the art of going wrong with confidence.

Indeed, many—perhaps even most—modern metaphysicians have been themselves unable to escape from such skepticism and have abandoned all attempt to maintain that the conclusions which they reach have any validity outside the limits of a game which they are playing or that they should be made the basis for the deduction of any principles of conduct. The subject matter of their science is, some say, not Reality but merely Possibility. They are concerned, not with what *is true,* but with what *would be true* if certain doubtful or perhaps false original propositions were granted, and their systems are, therefore, quite independent both of reality and of all other metaphysical systems which do not happen to assume the truth of the same premises chosen from the infinite number of possible ones. Thus various students of St. Thomas Aquinas admire him greatly (without embracing either the Roman Catholic or any other faith) simply because of the completeness with which he deduced a possible world from assumptions which they now believe false, and thus, in order to re-establish his credit in the world, they have been compelled to deprive him of the very claim which, more than any other, was responsible for the supreme importance attached to his work—of the claim, that is to say, that he deduced from principles eternally true rules for the conduct of temporal life.

Hence we may say that the metaphysical movement, in spite of all the subtlety which it has developed and in spite of the magnitude of the claims sometimes made for it, reveals a fatal tendency to disintegrate as soon as it is called upon to perform one of the chief functions of faith by furnishing a guide for conduct. When called upon to show how it may be made to do so, certain of its proponents like G. K. Chesterton and T. S. Eliot seek immediate refuge in Roman or Anglican Catholicism, whose dogmas, if accepted without argument, provide the basis which pure reason cannot discover. Those who are, on the other hand, unwilling or unable thus to abdicate in favor of an old and enfeebled religion are very likely to renounce for themselves the claims which the admirers of St. Thomas renounced for him and to say simply that the Science of Possibilities has no obligation to concern itself particularly with that one Possibility which happens to be Reality and which, as a matter of fact, it is quite willing to leave to those other sciences called Natural.

Thus the elaborate mental machinery which was

set in motion by the desire to escape from the stifling materialism of the modern world and which had as its purpose the establishment of the possibility that the natural and the human worlds are discontinuous has, as a matter of fact, actually succeeded in accomplishing very little since its chief results have been (1) to win for the old creeds a small number of troublesomely vacillating recruits and (2) considerably to increase the number of people interested in metaphysics considered rather as a game than as a means of arriving at truths relevant to the life which we live. The Middle Ages believed that it had laid its hands upon that phantom called Certitude, but when moderns set out to find it they discovered only Fictions which they might endeavor to render substantial but which persisted nevertheless in dissolving into thin air.

Perhaps it may be objected that the metaphysical movement is too new to be judged so quickly and so severely according to its accomplishment, but to one who has followed it not without desire for sympathetic understanding it must seem that it began to decay before it was completely formed. Certain minds, convinced that the triumphs of science were spiritually barren, set out to combat some of its deductions and to win for the humanistic conclusions of pure thought the right to assert the existence of spiritual verities denied or neglected by science. Instead of accomplishing this purpose the majority of these minds have ended, either by surrendering their freedom to dogmatic authority, or by retiring from the real world which they could not remold into some realm of Possibility whose purely fictional character they were willing to admit in exchange for the right to arrange those fictions into patterns more satisfactory than that which their triumphant enemy had revealed in all-embracing Nature. But when the subject matter of metaphysics is thus considered to be, not what *is* but what *might* be, it becomes pure art, and the admission that the human spirit finds a home in art alone is exactly the admission which distinguishes modern despair from that ancient optimism founded upon the belief that the scheme of nature corresponded in some way with the scheme, satisfactory to human desires, which was exposed in art and demonstrated by philosophy. Surrendering its pretensions so far as any ability to establish truths of reference are concerned and proclaiming itself essentially an art rather than a science, metaphysics, which promised so much, thus ends by confirming the very despair which it set out to combat.

EIGHT

Conclusion

I$_T$ is not by thought that men live. Life begins in organisms so simple that one may reasonably doubt even their ability to feel, much less think, and animals cling to or fight for it with a determination which we might be inclined to call superhuman if we did not know that a will to live so thoughtless and so unconditional is the attribute of beings rather below than above the human level. All efforts to find a rational justification of life, to declare it worth the living for this reason or that, are, in themselves, a confession of weakness, since life at its strongest never feels the need of any such justification and since the most optimistic philosopher is less optimistic than that man or animal who, his belief that life is good being too immediate to require the interposition of thought, is no philosopher at all.

In view of this fact it is not surprising that the subtlest intellectual contortions of modern metaphysics should fail to establish the existence of satisfactory aims for life when, as a matter of fact, any effort to do so fails as soon as it begins and can only arise as the result of a weakening of that self-justifying vitality which is the source of all life and of all optimism. As soon as thought begins to seek the "ends" or "aims" to which life is subservient it has already confessed its inability to achieve that animal acceptance of life for life's sake which is responsible for the most determined efforts to live and, in one sense, we may say that even the firmest medieval belief in a perfectly concrete salvation after death marks already the beginning of the completest despair, since that belief could not arise before thought had rendered primitive vitality no longer all-sufficient.

The decadent civilizations of the past were not saved by their philosophers but by the influx of simpler peoples who had centuries yet to live before their minds should be ripe for despair. Neither Socrates nor Plato could teach his compatriots any wisdom from which they could draw the strength to compete with the crude energy of their Roman neighbors, and even their thought inevitably declined soon after it had exhausted their vital energy. Nor could these Romans, who flourished longer for the very reason, perhaps, that they had slower and less subtle intellects, live forever; they too were compelled to give way in their time to barbarians innocent alike both of philosophy and of any possible need to call upon it.

The subhuman will to live which is all-sufficient for the animal may be replaced by faith, faith may be replaced by philosophy, and philosophy may attenuate itself until it becomes, like modern metaphysics, a mere game; but each of these developments marks a stage in a progressive enfeeblement of that will to live for the gradual weakening of which it is the function of each to compensate. Vitality calls upon faith for aid, faith turns gradually to philosophy for support, and then philosophy, losing all confidence in its own conclusions, begins to babble of "beneficent fictions" instead of talking about Truth; but each is less confident than what went before and each is, by consequence, less easy to live by. Taken together, they represent the successive and increasingly desperate expedients by means of which man, the ambitious animal, endeavors to postpone the inevitable realization that living is merely a physiological process with

only a physiological meaning and that it is most satis-
factorily conducted by creatures who never feel the
need to attempt to give it any other. But they are at
best no more than expedients, and when the last has
been exhausted there remains nothing except the possibility that the human species will be revitalized by
some race or some class which is capable of beginning
all over again.

Under the circumstances it is not strange that decadent civilizations are likely to think that the collapse of their culture is in reality the end of the
human story. Perhaps some of the last of the old
Roman intelligentsia realized that the future belonged
to the barbarians from the north and that it belonged
to them for the very reason that they were incapable
of assimilating ancient thought, but even among the
early Christian theologians there was a widespread
belief that the end of Rome could mean nothing except
the end of the world, and, for similar reasons, it is
difficult for us to believe in the possibility of anything
except either the continuation of modern culture or
the extinction of human life. But a glance at history
should make us hesitate before asserting that either
one of these alternative possibilities is likely to become
a reality. On the one hand all cultures have ultimately
collapsed and human life has, on the other hand, always persisted—not because philosophers have arisen
to solve its problems but because naïver creatures,
incapable of understanding the problems and hence
not feeling the need to solve them, have appeared
somewhere upon the face of the globe.

If modern civilization is decadent then perhaps it
will be rejuvenated, but not by the philosophers whose
subtlest thoughts are only symptoms of the disease
which they are endeavoring to combat. If the future
belongs to anybody it belongs to those to whom it has
always belonged, to those, that is to say, too absorbed
in living to feel the need for thought, and they will

come, as the barbarians have always come, absorbed
in the processes of life for their own sake, eating without asking if it is worth while to eat, begetting children without asking why they should beget them, and
conquering without asking for what purpose they conquer.

Doubtless even those among the last of the Romans
who had some dim conception of the fact that the
centuries immediately to follow would belong to the
barbarians were not, for the most part, greatly interested in or cheered by the fact. Thoughtful people
come inevitably to feel that if life has any value at all,
then that value lies in thought, and to the Roman it
probably seemed that it was hardly worth while to
save the human animal if he could be saved only by
the destruction of all that which his own ancestors
had achieved, and by the forgetting of everything
which he cared to remember. The annihilation of ancient culture was to him equivalent to the annihilation
of humanity, and a modern who has come to think in
a similar fashion can have only a languid interest in a
possible animal rejuvenation which would inevitably
involve a blunting of that delicate sensibility and that
exquisite subtlety of intellect upon which he has come
to set the very highest value.

But doubtless this ancient Roman speculated idly,
and it is impossible for us not to do the same.
Whence will the barbarians (and we may use that
word, not as a term of contempt but merely as a way
of identifying these people animated by vitally simple
thoughts) come? We are not surrounded as the
Romans were by childlike savages, and we can hardly
imagine the black tribes of Africa pushing in upon us.
Have we, within the confines of our own cities, popu-
lations quite as little affected by modern thought as
the Goths were affected by Greek philosophy, and
hence quite capable either of carrying peaceably on as
the aristocracy dies quietly off at the top or of arising

sometime to overwhelm us? Has China, having died
once, lain fallow long enough to have become once
more primitive, or are the Russians indeed the new
barbarians, even if they are such in a somewhat different sense than that implied in the sensational literature
of anti-Communist propaganda?

II

These Russians are young in the only sense of the
word which can have a meaning when applied to any
part of the human family. If all men had a common
ancestor, then all races are equally old in years, but
those which have never passed through the successive
and debilitating stages of culture retain that poten-
tiality for doing so which constitutes them racially
young, and the Russians, who have always lived upon
the frontiers of Europe, are in this sense a primitive
race, since European culture has never been for them
more than the exotic diversion of a small class. For
the first time in history the mass of the people is in
a position to employ its constructive faculties, and it
so happens that their domain is one which offers an
enormous field for the employment of such faculties.

Young races like young individuals need toys to
play with. Before the advent of the machine, the
Romans amused themselves with military and social
organization, pushing the boundaries of their empire
farther and farther back into unknown territory until
their energy was exhausted and they were compelled
to begin a gradual retraction; today, the processes of
industrial development are capable of absorbing much
of the vitality which could formerly find an outlet only
in conquest; but if modern people amuse themselves
by building factories or digging mines they do so for
exactly the same reason that the Romans annexed the
British Isles—because, that is to say, there is little
temptation to ask ultimate questions as long as there
are many tangible things to do and plenty of energy

to do them with. Russia has both, and for that very reason there is no other place in the world where one will find today an optimism so simple and so terrible.

We—particularly we in America—have done all that. We have dug our mines, piped our oil, built our factories, and, having done so, we have begun to settle down in our comfortable houses to ask what comes next. But the Russians are at least a century away from such a condition. They begin at a point at least as far back as we began a century ago and they are in the happy position of desiring certain things which they have good reason to believe ultimately achievable. Not only do they want to grow rich and to establish a form of society which will provide for an equitable distribution of their riches, but they find on every side some tangible task capable of being accomplished in such a way as to further their ambition. Perhaps when this ambition has been achieved, when all men are as materially comfortable as some few men are today, then the comfortable masses will discover what the comfortable few have discovered already, which is, of course, that comfort seems enough only when one happens not to have it. But that day is still long distant. Not only will the complete industrial development of the country occupy many years but the problems of the new society are themselves so complicated that they are not likely to be solved for generations and hence, in all probability, Russia will not grow ripe so rapidly as the United States did.

As a result of these conditions there has already developed in Russia a new philosophy of life which, in spite of the fact that it has taken a form influenced by modern industrial conditions, is easily recognizable as being essentially primitive in its simplicity. Sweeping aside the intellectual and emotional problems of Europe, refusing even in its art to concern itself with the psychology of the individual soul, Communism assumes that nothing is really important except those things upon which the welfare of the race depends, and in assuming that it is assuming exactly what a primitive society always assumes. Its drama and its poetry celebrate the machine exactly as the literature of a primitive people celebrates the process of hunting or of agriculture, and they do so for exactly the same reason, for the reason, that is to say, that agriculture on the one hand and industry on the other are the two fundamental processes by which the life of the people is sustained.

Communistic Utopianism is based upon the assumption that the only maladjustments from which mankind suffers are social in character and hence it is sustained by the belief that in a perfect state all men would be perfectly happy. Fundamentally materialistic, it refuses to remember that physical well-being is no guarantee of felicity and that, as a matter of fact, as soon as the individual finds himself in a perfectly satisfactory physical environment he begins to be aware of those more fundamental maladjustments which subsist, not between man and society but between the human spirit and the natural universe. And though, for this reason, it must seem to the cultivated European essentially naïve, yet in that very naïveté lies its strength as a social philosophy. Thanks to the fact that the perfect Communist is not aware of the existence of any problems more subtle than those involved in the production and distribution of wealth, he can throw himself into the business of living with a firm faith in the value of what he is doing and he can display an energy in practical affairs not to be equaled by anyone incapable of a similar belief in their ultimate importance.

All societies which have passed the first vigor of their youth reveal their loss of faith in life itself by the fact that they no longer consider such fundamental processes as other than means toward an end. Food, clothes, and warmth are considered merely as instruments, and the most eager attention is directed, not toward attaining them but toward the activities which men are at liberty to pursue when such fundamental things are granted. Productive labor is regarded as an evil, and when anything is said concerning the possibility of improving the condition of the masses, such improvement is always thought of as consisting essentially in so shortening even their hours of labor as to make possible for them also certain hours of freedom. Primitive societies, on the other hand, have no desire to escape from such fundamental processes. They do not hunt in order to live but they live in order to hunt, because for them the value of life lies in the activities necessary to carry it on; and the Communist philosophy of labor is based upon a similarly primitive outlook. Factories are considered, not as means toward an end but as ends in themselves. A full life is to consist, not in one spent in the pursuit of those thoughts or the cultivation of those emotions which are possible only when productive labor has been reduced to a minimum, but in one completely absorbed by such labor.

Hence it is that to the good Communist, as to the good tribesman, any question concerning the meaning of life is in itself completely meaningless and he will live the complicated industrial life of today exactly as the tribesman lives the simple life of his tribe—not in thought but in action. He has a sort of God, but his God is in reality what anthropologists call a culture-god; merely, that is to say, the spirit which presides over and infuses itself with the germination of the seed, the ripening of the fruit, or the whirring of the machine.

Such a philosophy comes nearer than any other to that unformulated one by which an animal lives. It does not ask any of the questions which a weary people inevitably ask and it is, as a matter of fact, less a system of thought than a translation into simple words of the will to live and thrive. But it is, for all that, only the more impressive as an evidence of the vigorous youth of the Russian mind. The visitor to Moscow who sees how eagerly its inhabitants live under conditions which are still very difficult, how gladly they accept both labor and, when necessary, privation, cannot but realize that they are sustained by a fundamental optimism unknown anywhere else in the world. At the present moment the inhabitants of many European countries *have* much more but they *hope* much less, and they are incapable of any acceptance of life so vital and so complete.

If the Communistic experiment is economically a failure, then these hopes may be soon disappointed; if it becomes economically a success, then they will doubtless still be disappointed in that more distant day when, the perfect state having been achieved, its inhabitants come to realize that the natural universe is as imperfectly adapted as ever to human needs. But man-the-animal lives in Time. A hope is a hope up to the instant when it is dashed, and the Russia of today is filled with a confidence hardly less elementary than that of the animal which, under the influence of the vital urge, acts as though the litter which it has just brought into the world were so tremendously worth saving that nothing else which had occurred since the dawn of the first day were of equal importance.

Perhaps, then, Europe has good reason to speak of the "Bolshevik menace," but if so the events which she fears are not quite the ones most likely to occur. If Russia or the Russian spirit conquers Europe it will not be with the bomb of the anarchist but with the vitality of the young barbarian who may destroy many things but who destroys them only that he may begin over again. Such calamities are calamitous only from the point of view of a humanism which values the complexity of its feelings and the subtlety of its intellect far more than Nature does. To her they are merely the reassertion of her right to recapture her own world, merely the process by which she repeoples the earth with creatures simple enough to live joyously there.

III

To us, however, such speculations as these are doubly vain. In the first place the future may belong, not to the Russians but to some class of people not yet thought of in this connection, and in the second place none of these possible futures is one which can have anything to do with us or our traditions. Though the new barbarians may forget we will remember that the paradox of humanism and the tragic fallacy are not to be altered by the establishment of new societies and that the despair which was the fruit of both ancient and modern civilization must inevitably ripen again in the course of the development of any society which enters upon the pursuit of human values.

Some critics of Communism have, to be sure, maintained that its tendencies were fundamentally antihuman and that, should it ever become established, it would so arrest the development of the humanistic spirit as to fix mankind forever in some changelessly efficient routine like that of an anthill. But even if this be true it does not alter the fact that its hopes are no hopes in which we can have any part, since we would be even more alien to such a society than to one which promised to recapitulate our own youth. The world may be rejuvenated in one way or another, but we will not. Skepticism has entered too deeply into our souls ever to be replaced by faith, and we can never forget the things which the new barbarians will never need to have known. This world in which an unresolvable discord is the fundamental fact is the world in which we must continue to live, and for us wisdom must consist, not in searching for a means of escape which does not exist but in making such peace with it as we may.

Nor is there any reason why we should fail to realize the fact that the acceptance of such despair as must inevitably be ours does not, after all, involve a misery so acute as that which many have been compelled to endure. Terror can be blacker than that and so can the extremes of physical want and pain. The most human human being has still more of the animal than of anything else and no love of rhetoric should betray one into seeming to deny that he who has escaped animal pain has escaped much. Despair of the sort which has here been described is a luxury in the sense that it is possible only to those who have much that many people do without, and philosophical pessimism, dry as it may leave the soul, is more easily endured than hunger or cold.

Leaving the future to those who have faith in it, we may survey our world and, if we bear in mind the facts just stated, we may permit ourselves to exclaim, a little rhetorically perhaps,

> Hail, horrors, hail,
> Infernal world! and thou profoundest hell,
> Receive thy new possessor.

If Humanism and Nature are fundamentally antithetical, if the human virtues have a definite limit set to their development, and if they may be cultivated only by a process which renders us progressively unfit to fulfill our biological duties, then we may at least permit ourselves a certain defiant satisfaction when we realize that we have made our choice and that we are resolved to abide by the consequences. Some small part of the tragic fallacy may be said indeed to be still valid for us, for if we cannot feel ourselves great as Shakespeare did, if we no longer believe in either our infinite capacities or our importance to the universe, we know at least that we have discovered the trick which has been played upon us and that whatever else we may be we are no longer dupes.

Rejuvenation may be offered to us at a certain price. Nature, issuing her last warning, may bid us embrace some new illusion before it is too late and accord ourselves once more with her. But we prefer rather to fail in our own way than to succeed in hers. Our human world may have no existence outside of our own desires, but those are more imperious than anything else we know, and we will cling to our own lost cause, choosing always rather to know than to be. Doubtless fresh people have still a long way to go with Nature before they are compelled to realize that they too have come to the parting of the ways, but though we may wish them well we do not envy them. If death for us and our kind is the inevitable result of our stubbornness then we can only say, "So be it." Ours is a lost cause and there is no place for us in the natural universe, but we are not, for all that, sorry to be human. We should rather die as men than live as animals.